Who the Hell is Jane Jacobs?

Who the hell is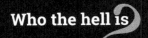

For students, teachers and curious minds, our **carefully structured jargon-free series** helps you really get to grips with brilliant intellectuals and their inherently complex theories.

Written in an **accessible and engaging** way, each book takes you through the **life and influences** of these brilliant intellectuals, before taking a deep dive into three of their **key theories in plain English.**

Smart thinking made easy!

POLITICS   PSYCHOLOGY   PHILOSOPHY   SOCIOLOGY   ART HISTORY

Who the Hell is Friedrich Nietzsche?

"...accessible and unambiguous... clarity and accuracy... highly recommend this book"

Jamie Corish, The Philosophy Foundation

Who the Hell is B.F. Skinner?

"...an outstanding biography of the man and his theories ...a must read"

Professor Sir Cary Cooper, CBE, University of Manchester

Who the Hell is Karl Marx?

"...accessible without losing any depth of analysis"

Judy Cox, *Socialist Review*

Who the Hell is Jean-Jacques Rousseau?

"...this is exactly what I need. Depth of analysis, yet written in an easily digestible style."

Jay, A level Philosophy teacher

Who the Hell is Karl Marx?

"...pulls Marx right out of that 'difficult' box into an accessible summary of his life and ideas."

Solomon Hughes, *Morning Star*

Who the Hell is Jane Jacobs?

And what are her theories all about?

Deborah Talbot

**BOWDEN
&BRAZIL**

First published in Great Britain in 2019 by
Bowden & Brazil Ltd
Felixstowe, Suffolk, UK.

British Library Cataloguing-in-Publication Data
A CIP record for this book is available from The British Library.

ISBN 978-1-9999492-2-8

To find out more about other books and authors in this series,
visit www.whothehellis.co.uk

Contents

Introduction

Cities are ever more central to human development. According to projections by the United Nation's World Population Prospects (2017), the global population will grow from around 7.6 billion in 2019 to just over 11 billion by 2030. Urbanization is one of the most significant trends of contemporary society, yet it has received scant attention from government as a distinct social phenomenon.

Some of the key issues facing societies across the world – pollution, economic growth, housing, inequality, immigration, to name but a few – are all issues that either happen in cities or are caused by the way we organize cities.

Let's consider the problem of pollution. Whereas in the near past, pollution was caused by industrial production for the most part, today it is largely caused by consumption; specifically our preferred mode of transportation, the car. Cars have been increasingly dominating the city from the time they were first commercially available in the early 20th century, far outstripping investment in public transport. Figures by Statista (2018) show that car sales globally have more than doubled over the last 30 years.

Did successive governments in advanced industrial nations, when they legislated to expand roadways into the cities and cut back on public transport innovations, foresee that our urban areas would become choked by exhaust fumes? Possibly. Perhaps they were merely tempted and seduced by the growing power of the car manufacturers, who promised jobs and good wages before moving production to cheaper countries. Regardless of the motivations, the consequences have been that cities are fundamentally changed by the car, arguably for the worse and without justifiable reason.

For each successive social problem we look at in our cities, it's possible to see a corresponding clash between the actual nature of cities – how they work – and national government policy and ideology. Essentially, what this clash comes down to is whether we see cities as being made for people or to satisfy ideologies.

This book is about Jane Jacobs – urbanist, activist and pioneer – and it is part of a series of books entitled 'Who the hell is?' Her place in this series is well-deserved as Jacobs was possibly the most influential thinker on cities in the 20th century. She had plenty of answers to the problems mentioned in this introduction, as this book sets out to illustrate. And if we were to ask her whether cities are made by people or ideas, she'd probably say both, in so far as cities and ideas are made by people.

But although Jacobs has global admirers, still she remains an underrated thinker. This may be largely due to the fact that most of her arguments go against some of the central tenets of profit-orientated property development seen in large cities during her lifetime and today. There is nothing about contemporary governmental ideas that celebrates small, human-scaled development of the sort she would advocate.

Jacobs' writing is so original that it is hard to place in a canon. Since a 'canon' is a body of ideas recognized by academia as forming a tradition, any ideas that are generated outside of academia are unlikely to be absorbed into that hallowed tradition. Jacobs was an outsider, whose perceptive insights were drawn from experience as much as theory, so her ideas cannot be seen to neatly fit into the canon or tradition of urbanism and planning. So it seems especially important to introduce her ideas to a global audience though this new series of books.

It is ironic that Jacob's ideas haven't become more influential, when we consider the endless mistakes and messes political leaders make of cities. Urbanism remains a small and discreet subject, and we tend to think of it as the home of high-powered and elitist architects. Planners, who are often hard-pressed and underfunded, are less guided by ideas and research as they bounce from one highly complicated development to another. Residents who are often impacted by large-scale development simply feel it is all beyond them. Jane Jacobs aimed to change all of that, and show us that everyone can, and should, have a say.

Who the Hell is Jane Jacobs? aims to show how Jacobs' ideas about cities and the economy evolved. In order to do this, we must look at who she was as a person, where and how she lived, and how her ferocious intellect led her to unchartered frontiers of thought. This book therefore explores her life and influences before going on to distil her writings into three concepts, talking along the way about how these ideas play out in contemporary society. It hopes to show that we need to rethink how we plan, construct, change and live in cities, and to remind ourselves, as Jane Jacobs herself instructed, that society is about people, not money or power.

1. Jacobs' Life Story

Urbanism and architecture have always been elite businesses – very male dominated (and middle or upper-class white male at that). Jane Jacobs broke through it all at a time when women were very much on the back foot, without even needing to make an issue out of her gender: 'She didn't assert herself as a feminist, she just was one [...] she was an uncommonly strong and self-confident woman never afraid to air her views or exhibit her reliably superior intellect' (Kanigel, 2016).

Even though her interest was in cities and economics, she was not shy of being forthright on the position of women. She was very keen to refocus people's attention on the important work that women did, from protesting to organizing to writing. When talking about the tendency to use the inclusive pronoun of 'man', she says:

> 'I don't like it, because we get a distorted view of who has been doing all those things. Women have been doing them, too, and they're just as important.' (Kanigel, 2016)

Her point is that women – whether they are playing a traditional nurturing and family role or breaking out to live a more intellectual life, or doing both of these – play an active role in city and social life. It is our gaze that is misdirected to give men's activities prominence. She goes on:

> 'Like other women who are neither dolts nor masochists, I have always recognized that society is based on a tissue of outright lies about the inferiority of women (and others who are not men of Western European descent) and the natural superiority of men. I have not made this an overt cause, but have simply acted as if it is not true, trusting that falsity destroys itself eventually.' (2005, quoted in Kanigel, 2016)

Jacobs' work has been extremely influential on women urbanists. Planning and architecture is still dominated by men. Statistics from the UK (RIBA, cited in White, 2012) showed that the number of women in architecture fell from 28 per cent to 21 per cent between 2009 and 2011. A 'Women in Architecture' survey also showed that two-thirds of women in the profession in the UK suffered sex discrimination (White, 2012).

Does it matter if women can't influence the built environment? According to Jane Jacobs, it does. It's still the case that men and women lead remarkably different lives, even as so many women work today. They are more subject to violent assault and harassment in public, which influences how they use the city. And they are more likely to be looking after children, which influences their mobility and how they use spaces.

And there are differences in other ways too, such as how they think about cities. In a debate between developer James Rouse and Jane Jacobs in 1980 at the Boston Great Cities Conference, they discussed whether cities should be built with big ideas and visions rather than small and incremental change. Rouse cited Daniel Burnham, who said: 'Make no little plans, for they have no magic to stir men's blood'. Jacobs retorted: 'Funny, big plans never stirred women's blood. Women have always been willing to consider little plans' (Jacobs cited in Gratz, 2011). Her point was that women tend to be more pragmatic and less egoistic and wasteful, perhaps even more collaborative and accepting of difference (Johnston-Zimmerman, 2018). A series of small plans, each carved out in the spaces between a host of other responsibilities, could make for a lively, imaginative and diverse environment.

Jacobs didn't just study city life from afar; she lived it and loved it. She was her work. It is for this reason that it is essential that we first take a look at her life and how she lived it in order to understand how she developed her ideas to become the inspirational woman that she did.

Fig. 1 Jane Jacobs brandishing documentary evidence in her fight to save the West Village in New York in 1961.

A Happy Childhood

Jane Jacobs (née Jane Isabel Butzner) was born in Scranton, Pennsylvania, on 16 May 1916. She was the third child of John Decker Butzner, a doctor, and Bess Robison Butzner, who trained as a teacher but later became a nurse. She grew up with three siblings – her elder sister, Betty, and two brothers, John and Jim – all of whom she would remain close to throughout her life. A fifth Butzner child, William, was born three years after Betty, but tragically died at the age of two.

The Butzner children grew up in the leafy suburb of Dunmore, in an impressive house with porch columns, gables and cornices, and a large garden at the back. Jane described it as 'a cheerful place' where the family 'did a lot of talking'. She was close to her father, sharing the same intellectually curious traits. The two of them would often sit together looking through one of her father's encyclopedias, Jane looking at the drawings and plates, while her father read out interesting facts. Having less in common with her mother, Jane nonetheless admired her hugely: her compassion, her intelligence and her principles.

As a child, Jane read prolifically – anything she could get her hands on. She had imaginary conversations with historical figures to avoid boredom. She let her imagination run wild, readily believing in all the local myths, and she wrote poetry by the reams, even succeeding in getting some of them published when she was a teenager. She was also an active Girl Scouts member, enjoying the camps, astronomy, tree finding and the many crafts.

Her upbringing was freer and more unconventional than most, and her father, in particular, encouraged his children to think for themselves and to believe that they could do anything they wanted. Jane describes her parents as never undermining their children, and as a consequence, a healthy self-esteem accompanied her throughout her life.

While her upbringing was solidly middle-class, her family did not escape the impact of economic decline. Scranton, once a lively and thriving metropolis, began to stagnate when Jane was a teenager, and this made her think hard about why some cities prospered while others floundered. She was perhaps protected from the worst of the depression of the 1930s though, and her resilient attitude helped her with any difficulties that she did face.

A Difficult Education

Despite her intelligence, Jane hated school, deploring its attitude towards freethinking and creativity, which was at such odds with her home life. At both her schools – first George Washington in Dunmore and then Central High in Scranton – Jane went with an attitude of resistance. Schools at that time, she argued, were 'more regimented than they are now. For hours we would sit there doing this or that and we wouldn't be allowed to talk unless we were asked a question' (Kanigel, 2016). It was so bad that she developed a small tic in her throat in the classroom – a little noise – just so she could reassure herself that she could still talk. By the time she was in third grade, she was sneaking books into school to read rather than listen to her teachers.

She often got into trouble for speaking her mind. When Jane was seven, her teacher told the class to promise to clean their teeth every day for the rest of their lives. But only the previous day, Dr Butzner had told Jane never to promise to do anything for the rest of her life – she was too young. So Jane refused to promise in the class and told her classmates not to promise either. Her teacher lost her temper and threw Jane out of the classroom. No mention was made of the incident when she returned to school – Jane had won.

Despite hating school, Jane's high school was in the city, which was to open up another world to her. Suddenly she had access to plays, lectures and bigger libraries. She was able to see the city up close and explore under her own steam. She continued to be a dreamer, racking up zeros in the 'late' column of the school register. Begging her mother for a note to explain her lateness one day, Bess obliged, writing 'Jane sat too long at the edge of the bed with one shoe in her hand' (Kanigel, 2016), a pastime of getting caught up in her thoughts that would never leave her. High school also gave Jane the opportunity to join the school literary magazine, *Impressions*, becoming the poetry editor and interviewing various literary figures.

Jane graduated from high school in 1933 at the height of the Great Depression with 12 million people out of work and an unemployment rate of 24 percent. Her parents and the circumstances encouraged in her a pragmatic attitude to work – that is, to find something practical that earns you money while also pursuing what you wanted to do. Jane wanted to write, but she also needed to earn money, so she signed up for a secretarial course at the Powell School of Business and trained to be a stenographer (someone who can do shorthand to record speech quickly; this is a skill still used by many journalists today). Shortly afterwards, Jane took on an internship at *The Scranton Republican* newspaper, writing short articles for the section 'Women's Society and Club News'. Jane described the newspaper as her 'journalism school'.

In May 1934, Jane was sent by her parents to stay with her Aunt Martha for three months in Higgins, North Carolina – a remote place up in the mountains. 'My parents thought I should get a good look at a very different and interesting kind of life', she says (Kanigel, 2016). Her aunt was a force of nature all of her own: driven, intelligent and a woman on a mission. She was certainly a positive influence on Jane. We will look at this episode in Jane's life in more detail in Chapter 2.

New York, New York

In November 1934 Jane moved to New York City, where she would live for the next 34 years. At 18 years old, she was tall and rather striking-looking, with prominent cheekbones, fine straight brown hair with hints of red, round glasses and a half-smile that gave the impression she was constantly hiding a joke. She loved New York, calling it a 'wonder', but at the time of arriving work was scarce. She spent her mornings looking for work and her afternoons getting off the subway at random stops so that she could explore the city. After various short-lived, badly paid secretarial jobs, she found herself one afternoon in Manhattan's fur district, which caught her attention and would turn out to be the beginning of her writing career. Captivated by the comings and goings of the fur trade, Jane wrote a 1,000-word story called 'Where the Fur Flies' which was accepted by the editor of *Vogue* – quite a feat for a 19-year-old high-school graduate. She wrote three more articles for *Vogue*, while taking classes at NYU in magazine, feature and editorial writing. She later took classes in economic geography, psychology, geology, zoology and constitutional law at Columbia University's continuing studies program (though she never graduated) and loved them all. Improbably, her class in constitutional law provided her with the material for her first book, *Constitutional Chaff; Rejected Suggestions of the Constitutional Convention of 1787* – a compilation of rejected ideas that reflected her love for the contrary.

Jane's love of getting off the train at a random subway station led her to discover the area of New York City where she would live for the next three decades. All three places where she lived were within 450 m (500 yd) of Christopher Street subway station: a place that captured her interest and kindled her lifelong love of urban communal living. The diversity of the people, the shops, the houses; the irregularities, the ambiguities, the very soul of the community living there captivated Jane and compelled her to

Fig. 2 Manhattan was viewed by Jacobs as the ideal mixture of dense living with shops below and wide sidewalks. But the skyscrapers loom and creep as land becomes hyper-inflated.

move there with her sister so that she could be in the heart of it all. It is easy to imagine this discovery as a catalyst for her work.

In 1940, Jane got her first real break – a job at the trade magazine for the metals industry, *Iron Age*. She was hired as a secretary, and then went on to write and edit articles, finally becoming Associate Editor. In 1943, she got a job at The US Office of War Information (OWI) writing propaganda, which eventually lead, in 1946, to a job at the government publication *Amerika*, where she would work until 1952.

Marriage and Children

It was during this time that Jane met Robert Hyde Jacobs Jr., the son of an engineer who had grown up in New Jersey. Bob (as he was known) had studied architecture at university but with the onset of war had ended up working for a company called Grumman, designing aircraft components – one particularly curious one being a gadget that allowed the pilot's urine to flow out of the plane while he was flying. With the war still raging on, Bob worked all hours before returning to his rented room in a house on Long Island. An intelligent, gentle man with dark, curly hair and small round spectacles, he very quickly became smitten with Jane when they met at a party in March 1944. It was only a week later that he proposed. After initially turning him down, Jane changed her mind the following week, receiving an engagement ring made from a hose clamp from the Grumman workshop. In May that same year, two weeks before D-day, they were married at Jane's childhood home in Scranton, before going off on honeymoon on a cycling trip around Pennsylvania and New York State – a pastime that Jane became known for.

By all accounts, Bob and Jane had an incredibly close relationship. Sharing ideas and insights, they were best friends and confidants. They moved to Hudson Street in the West Village in 1948 into a crumbling three-storey house, which had previously been a candy store. The area could have passed for a slum, surrounded by dilapidated warehouses, small industrial businesses, and the noise that went with it. They had to completely refurbish the house inside and out, but with Bob's architectural and design skills, Hudson Street was turned into a quirky, comfortable home. Their first child was born a few months after moving in – a son named James Kedzie, but known as Jim. A second son, Edward Decker, came along two years later, and a daughter, Mary, three years after that. Turning her back on the conventional housewife's fate, Jane continued to work while raising her three children. Glennie Lenear, an African-American woman who worked for the family for a dozen years, helped Jane with the children and the housework, until her death in 1960.

The Jacobs were a close, unorthodox family. The children referred to their parents as 'Jane' and 'Bob', rather than Mom and Dad. Jane and Bob always treated their children like adults, talking to them on the same level as to each other. Topics of conversation around the kitchen table typically involved politics, archaeology, architecture, or whatever else had captured Jane's attention at the time. They had a relaxed parenting style, believing in 'thinking things through' and leaving the children to learn from experience, rather than yelling and remonstrating. They all had a pair of green mechanic's overalls, which they wore around the house – this being the 'working uniform' of choice for Jane and her son Jim, in particular.

Becoming an Urbanist

Bob and Jane's shared interest in the city and its buildings became apparent during Jane's time at *Amerika*, where she wrote her first article on urban dwellings. Titled 'Planned Rebuilding of Run-down Urban Areas', it was Jane's first real study of run-down neighbourhoods and, while she would later disagree with some of the opinions she expressed in this piece, it was a subject that was to capture her completely for the rest of her life.

In 1952, Jane followed up on her evolving interest in architecture by getting a job at *Architectural Forum*. She saw her role as beginning on a positive note when she was asked to choose which 'beat' she would like to take as editor – hospitals and schools or private homes – rather than just being told what she would be working on. She chose the former, and Bob taught her how to read blueprints in the evenings when the children had gone to bed. It was at the *Forum* that she began to develop an urbanist narrative and, for the first time, was given free rein to express her opinions. Perhaps inspired by Jane's articles on hospitals and the design problems they posed, Bob ended up devoting his architectural career to designing hospitals, working on a few dozen, including the Hadassah-Hebrew University Hospital in Jerusalem.

Rebel and Activist

It wasn't until 1955 that Jane began to question the cities, streets and buildings, plans and architectural visions that she had been writing about. It was at this time that she met an Episcopal minister, the Rev. William H. Kirk, who was overseeing the revitalization of East Harlem. He toured the area with her on many occasions, and (as she notes in the introduction to her book, *The Death and Life of Great American Cities*, 1961) first implanted in her the idea that it was important 'to try to begin understanding the intricate social and economic order under the seeming disorder of cities'. She goes on, 'By showing me East Harlem, [he] showed me a way of seeing other neighborhoods, and downtowns too.'

When Jacobs was asked to write an article on Philadelphia's redevelopment program, she began to be troubled by the discrepancy between the idealistic plans for a city and the gritty realism of the resulting project. The following year an opportunity arose for her to give voice to her thoughts. The Urban Design conference had invited the *Architectural Forum* editor, Doug Haskell, to give a talk, but as he was unable to attend, he put forward Jane's name to replace him. Terrified at first at the idea of speaking in front of 200 people, Jane finally acquiesced on the proviso that she could speak about a topic of her choice. She spoke on the subject that she would become known for: the importance of the community; how shabby, low-rent spaces were vital for a thriving neighbourhood, how they allowed a myriad of independent stores and community organizations to survive for the benefit of everyone.

Jane's talk was a resounding success and went some way to making her a name in her field. Certainly it resulted in her being given higher-profile assignments at the *Forum*, many of which would now carry her byline (where previously they had been published anonymously). One in particular was her article 'Downtown is for People', which appeared in April 1958 as part of a series on problems in the city. The article was published to great acclaim and would later turn into her book *The Death and Life of Great American Cities*, thanks to a Rockefeller Foundation grant and a leave of absence from *Forum*. Though she visited many areas while she was writing the book, such as the urban renewal projects of St. Louis and Boston, the book is based on her intimate connection to New York – the place where she raised her children, let them play on the sidewalks, and where she cycled to work and chatted to neighbours. It took Jane over two years to write *Death and Life*, which would finally give her wide recognition and led to a flood of requests for various publications, many of which she turned down. It would later be named as one of the principal books for the American Association of University Women.

Even during her period of intense writing Jane became involved with various city planner battles. She became a community activist from the mid to late 1950s, at which time her home in Greenwich Village, New York, was under threat from the planners and city levellers, who wanted to build a road through Washington Square Park. Jacobs and other residents formed a committee – the Joint Emergency Committee to Close Washington Square to Traffic – and eventually she won by securing the backing of assemblyman Carmine DeSapio who was up for re-election. They did this by stroking his ego as a powerful man, threatening to back his opponent, and then holding a rally to show their strength. They also had a petition with 35,000 signatures. Jane and her fellow activists won. The park remains open today.

Her protagonist in this fight was a man who wanted to build roads all over Greenwich Village – Robert Moses – whom we will talk about more in the next chapter. Tellingly, he was filled with rage at Jane and her group. 'There is nobody against this,' he is reported to have said, 'NOBODY, NOBODY, NOBODY, but a bunch of, a bunch of MOTHERS' (Kanigel, 2016). But mothers, much like youth, it seems, can change the world.

Jane had many fights like this, from preventing slum clearance to battling against roads. Between 1958 and 1962 alone she became embroiled in the fight to save East Harlem, Washington Square Park, the sidewalks (pavements) of Hudson Street and then Hudson Street itself, which had been earmarked for urban renewal. Jane, along with friends and neighbours, spent a year fighting, which involved telephone calls, letters, hearings, legal papers, presentations, petitions and rallies. She describes that time as being so hectic that she 'just disconnected the doorbell and left the door open at night so we could work and people could come and go' (Kanigel, 2016). Then came the Lower Manhattan Expressway project the following year. Jacobs not only wrote about problems in the cities, she actively involved herself at every opportunity – she really did live her work. While she may not have had the same academic qualifications as many of her peers, she probably had more first-hand experience than all of them put together.

As Jacobs herself said in an interview with Roberta B. Gratz, 'I couldn't believe there would've been this much stupidity about New York' (Jacobs, 1978). When *Death and Life* was published in 1961, of course, something changed and the tide turned against the unopposed razing of neighbourhoods to suit the planning idealists and car lovers. Still there were fights to be had and neighbourhoods to be preserved, but Jane wasn't an outsider anymore. Her voice carried weight. The Lower Manhattan

Expressway project was rejected in December 1962 but by April 1968 the threat of the expressway was back, and this time the backers were the New York State Department of Transportation. At a crucial hearing, Jane pushed her way onto the stage, later getting herself arrested. Only four months previously, Jane had been arrested at an anti-war protest, alongside Susan Sontag: 'I'm afraid you will have a jailbird daughter' she wrote to her mother. Her son Ned's reaction was equally humorous: 'You know, for a woman of 53, you lead a very exciting life' (Kanigel, 2016).

Moving to Canada

In June 1968 the Jacobs moved to Toronto, Canada, to prevent her two sons from being drafted into the Vietnam War. They left without telling anyone, due to Jane still being under indictment from her arrest in April. Piling into an old VW bus, the Jacobs packed up their things and headed north. They hadn't even finished unpacking before the whole family found themselves thrown into a city fight against an expressway that was to be built right through the street they had just moved on to – Spadina Road. While the Jacobs did not get involved through choice (the fight would take two years) it was perhaps just what they needed in order to properly settle in to their adopted country. It gave them the opportunity to meet many interesting and fearless people, and it placed Jane exactly where she wanted to be. That same year saw her invited onto a Canadian television programme on urban design and some months later she wrote an article called 'A City Getting Hooked on the Expressway Drug' for *The Globe and Mail*. She even teamed up with the University of Toronto professor, Marshall McLuhan, to make a film about the future expressway. *The Burning Would* (sic) was effective and went on to be shown all over Canada and even the USA (and is available today on YouTube).

The expressway battle gave her access to the city government through the political figures that she met – something she'd never had in New York. Toronto's mayor, David Crombie, was well aware of who Jacobs was, having taught *Death and Life* during his time as a university professor. He was all for rejuvenating slum areas without razing them to the ground and starting again. He describes Jane as 'legitimizing our instincts [...] She gave a moral legitimacy to us' (Kanigel, 2016). St. Lawrence in Toronto was one such project that had the Jacobs stamp all over it, which we will look at in more detail in Chapter 2.

In 1970, the Jacobs finally found a home on Albany Avenue, where Jane would live for the rest of her life. It was a large three-story redbrick house that had originally been built in 1910 for William Arthur Park, a University of Toronto paleontologist, and which Bob completely transformed into a wonderful family home. In 1974, Jane became a Canadian citizen and very much established in her neighbourhood. She worked doggedly on her books over the next three decades, publishing ten in her lifetime, all of which played their own specific part in her intellectual development.

In 1996, Jane was awarded a medal from the University of Virginia, with Bob by her side. But sadly, a few months later, they found out that Bob had terminal lung cancer and he died in September of that same year. Jane survived her husband by a decade, determined to keep writing right up until the end of her life. When she finally left this world on the 25 April 2006 her family issued the following statement:

'What's important is not that she died but that she lived, and that her life's work has greatly influenced the way we think. Please remember her by reading her books and implementing her ideas.' (Kanigel, 2016)

Jane Jacobs' Timeline

Jane Jacobs

1916	Jane Jacobs is born in Scranton, Pennsylvania
1934	Moves to New York City
1941	Publishes *Constitutional Chaff: rejected suggestions of the Constitutional Convention*
1943	Begins working at The US Office of War Information (OWI), writing propaganda
1945	Made redundant, begins freelancing
1946	Begins working at Amerika, writing propaganda for readers in the Soviet Union
1961	Publishes *The Death and Life of Great American Cities*

World Events

1914 -19	World War I
1920	Women get the vote in America
1929	Global economic collapse leading to the Great Depression
1938	World War II breaks out
1941	Japan bombs Pearl Harbor bringing the USA into the war and bringing employment to America, particularly for women
1945	With the end of WWII, employment returns to pre-war levels
1946	The Cold War begins between the Soviet Union & the Eastern Bloc and the US & its allies
1961	US President John Kennedy sends troops to Vietnam to counter the Viet Cong

1967	Arrested at an anti-Vietnam-war protest		
1968	Moves to Toronto, Canada		
1969	Publishes *The Economy of Cities*	**1969**	US government holds the first Vietnam War draft lottery
1974	Becomes a Canadian citizen	**1974**	Vietnam war ends
1980	Publishes *The Question of Separatism: Quebec and the Struggle over Sovereignty*	**1980**	Referendum on independence for Quebec fails, but precipitates constitutional change
1984	Publishes *Cities and the Wealth of Nations*	**1981**	Ronald Reagan becomes US president, marking the beginning of laissez-faire capitalism (which has a big impact on cities)
1992	Publishes *Systems of Survival*		
		1994	The North American Free Trade Agreement (NAFTA) comes into effect
2000	Publishes *The Nature of Economies*		
2004	Publishes *Dark Age Ahead*		

2. Influences on Jacobs' Thinking

Some writers have clear intellectual lineages. You can see who or what their main influences are and how they as writers have enhanced, in a small way, a particular theoretical or practical heritage. Not so with Jane Jacobs. Like other female writers at the time – Betty Friedan, Rachel Carson, Doris Lessing (who also did not have much by way of a formal education) – Jane Jacobs was forging her own path, often in the face of public attempts by men to humiliate and control her.

Not that she was interested in noticing. Like all pioneers, Jacobs' personality – argumentative, outspoken and intellectually curious – allowed her to shift the critical gaze to one side in the single-minded pursuit of her ideas. Although she was an activist and a mother, for a generous portion of the day she went to her office to work on her writing. And like most writers forging new paths, the source of her inspiration was the expanse of her own mind.

Yet there were people, places and events that did influence her. Even the most committed writers on a very distinctive mission have key moments in their lives when a person or an event disrupts and throws them onto another train of thought. For Jane Jacobs, that might be a positive influence or simply someone or something she decided to argue with.

This chapter will look at just some of these, before exploring, in a broad brush, how she influenced others.

Family

It goes without saying that our families influence us. But for Jacobs, some of her family connections actively fed her intellectual development. One of these was Martha Robinson, Jacobs' aunt, who moved to the town of Higgins, North Carolina in 1928, at the age of 48. Higgins was a small community that had gone into steep decline – poverty, alcoholism, lack of schooling and the ongoing loss of basic skills were some of the problems that had begun to impoverish the town. Martha decided to stay and rebuild its community resources, starting with a Sunday school, bible classes, church plays and fundraising. She also got philanthropic funding to build a new community centre for a library and craft workshops. Local people responded by relearning skills they had lost, and as a result the area became known for its arts and crafts in the later 20th century (showing that the 'vital little plans' that architect Daniel Burnham had so derided – really do shape the future). Jane stayed with her aunt for six months in 1934 after leaving school.

What Aunt Martha achieved was inspirational. But the way it influenced Jacobs was by giving her insights into how, when communities are cut off from civilization and commerce, they can easily drift into decline. Areas descend into torpor, and useful skills can be quickly lost. Parallels can be seen in former coal-mining villages in the UK, where many among the population, having lost the main source of livelihood, fell into drug addiction (in 2003, one in three families were found to be affected). Or in remote seaside towns, all around the world, where tourism fails for one reason or another and suddenly there is no work and no possibility of accessing work. In these situations of sudden mass unemployment, people become ill, passive and hopeless, accepting a spiralling loss of aspiration.

In her book, *Cities and the Wealth of Nations* (1984), Jacobs wrote about her aunt's town, Higgins, in the chapter 'Bypassed Places', but called it 'Henry' to disguise it slightly. She reflected on this issue of economic, social and cultural decline, and in the case of Henry, she argued it was because it had no connection to the dynamism of a nearby city because of geographical remoteness.

We are prone to romanticize the rural, but Jacobs did not think rural areas were idyllic. She saw the flaws of these places: despite their natural beauty, they did not contain the elements people needed to maintain and advance civilization. In her later work, for example *Dark Age Ahead* (2004), she became preoccupied with the end of civilization. Perhaps her experience of Higgins gave her some insight into how that collapse might take place.

Jacobs was also, arguably, influenced by both her husband, Bob, and her children. As we saw in Chapter 1, Bob and Jane shared a lot of the same interests, particularly when it came to their environment, and they inspired and helped one another throughout their lives. Their children also played an important role in their lives: children teach their parents to see the world through different eyes and can help them to understand how different experiences are depending on 'who's looking'; that is to say, the perspective of the person. It was, perhaps, Jacobs' children who taught her the value of Washington Square Park and which put her in contact with other mothers with whom she fought battles against Robert Moses. Certainly her children were what influenced her to move to Toronto. Were she not trying to enable her sons to escape the draft, her life may never have taken that turn, and what Toronto offered her in terms of an opportunity to positively assert her ideas would go on to become an important part of her work (see Chapter 3).

Urbanists and Sociologists

Arguably there was no specific intellectual influence working on Jane Jacobs. She had a few mentors at *Architecture Forum*, but to a great extent, as Kanigel notes, her work is about propelling herself beyond what she produced for that publication. She discussed and tussled with many a theorist, but her ideas developed often in opposition to them. In an interview with James Kunstler in *Metropolis*, she said this:

> '*In* The Death and Life of Great American Cities, *I have a whole list of people who I acknowledge receiving help from, but it's not intellectual help...I admired some of the people I worked with at* Architecture Forum. *And William H. ["Holly"] Whyte. He was a friend of mine. He was an important person to me, and he was somebody whose ideas…yes, we were on the same wavelength. And it was through Holly that I met Jason [Epstein], and he became my publisher...I liked my editor and still do.*' (Jacobs, 2001)

Whyte was an ethnographer (someone who studies people and cultures) who was most famous for his book *The Organization Man* (1956). He was also considered an urbanist who specialized in observing people in urban settings, writing, for example, *The Social Life of Small Urban Spaces* (1980). He founded the Street Life Project, which analyzed human behaviour and the dynamics of the street, making important observations about how pedestrians actually used space. This stance closely aligned with Jacobs' emphasis on walking the streets and observing how cities (and the people within them) really worked.

However, as someone who wasn't actively engaged in academic life (and often was quite dismissive of its value), Jacobs was as likely to find inspiration from a shopkeeper or a community activist as from the leading theorists of her time. One such activist was William Kirk, who she met in 1955. Kirk headed up the Union Settlement in East Harlem, New York, which provided health and social services to the area. During his time in East Harlem he'd seen the human scale tenements being replaced by high-rise towers, which he felt (though he had no hard evidence) was to the detriment of the community. Jacobs worked with him through her role at *Architectural Forum*, and he offered to take her on a tour of his patch, which she did often. Through his eyes, she began to see that the area wasn't a disordered slum, but a place with its own social order, its own commerce and its own sense of community. She understood that the tearing down of the so-called slums actually meant the destruction of retail and commercial space and the ripping apart of the delicate social order. Of course, not everyone would have listened to Kirk, or opened their eyes to what he wanted to show them. But Jane Jacobs did.

Ultimately, Jacobs' collaboration with Kirk in East Harlem did not prevent wholesale 'renewal'. Two thousand businesses were lost, along with plenty of viable tenement housing (Alexiou,

2006). But her involvement actively changed how she looked at the city, and in a way that proved valuable for Greenwich Village and later Toronto.

Jacobs read widely and almost anything that piqued her interest, from economics to sociology to philosophy. She absorbed quantitative and qualitative data. This perhaps accounted for the highly imaginative, original and almost maverick (in a positive sense) quality to her writing. But most importantly, reading widely and critically allowed her to escape what her friend Whyte would call 'groupthink', where people would be trapped within an intellectual and social framework – a way of seeing and thinking – defined by a single canon or institution.

Jacobs recognized that groupthink is possibly the most important flaw of city planners: they have not been trained to trust their own eyes and judgement or to think outside of a very narrow framework. In Jacobs' time, this framework was the concept of urban renewal.

Planners

Planners were Jane Jacobs' main protagonists. It was they who prioritized the 'slum' clearance of the tenements, they who proposed new roads and expressways through the intimate city streets, and they who refused to acknowledge the importance of systems of micro-commerce. There was no one who symbolized this perspective more than Robert Moses, the 'master builder' of New York and its suburbs in the mid-20th century. Despite their rare entanglement, Moses and Jacobs were in opposition to one another, epitomizing two different visions of New York, as Kanigel argues:

'...two memorable figures, tied to diametrically opposing visions of New York. Moses, the man of plans, maps and models, the reshuffling of whole urban landscapes, the destruction of neighborhoods, wielder of marionette strings of power; Jane Jacobs, all by herself in her writing studio, lured onto the urban battlefield only by existential challenges to her home, protective of her streets and sidewalks against the dark forces of unbridled power.' (Kanigel, 2017)

This description doesn't really get to the substantial reasons for Jacobs' opposition to Moses' plans. So what did Moses stand for, and why was it so meaningful and problematic to Jacobs?

Before World War II, Moses had been a social welfare campaigner and progressive, keen to tackle the kind of poverty revealed by the Great Depression. Post-war he managed to accumulate a great deal of power and the ability to harness large amounts of public funding through holding many and various unelected city-based state titles, such as President of the Long Island State Parks Commission and New York City Planning Commissioner. His idealism had, as it so often does, turned into power and control as he tried to make people bend to his will and vision. He is known for quoting the proverb that epitomizes all budding autocrats: 'You can't make an omelette without breaking eggs' (Moses, quoted in the movie *Citizen Jane*, 2016).

Moses was old-fashioned in the way that he saw cars and driving as a form of leisure, hence he was committed to the building of freeways inside and outside the city. Jacobs, on the other hand, wrote extensively against designing cities around cars.

Moses favoured the separation of the city's different functions: he saw housing, leisure and parks as all occupying different spaces. For example, during his period in office he built 658 playgrounds, which were to take children off the streets. He favoured high-rise residences, further separating the nature of living from the streets. This separation of function was something that Jacobs wrote critically about in *Death and Life*. She believed that uses (residential, retail, industry, and so on) should be mixed up and integrated. To do otherwise – as she noted in her extensive writings on one Moses project, the Lincoln Centre – would be to create 'dead zones' where no other commercial activity could be generated.

Most people think playgrounds are a wonderful thing, and their style and safety are much debated by parents. Yet Jacobs, in the chapter 'The uses of sidewalks: assimilating children' in *Death and Life*, wondered whether children got more fun out of the everyday life we see in the streets. As she argued:

> *'Why do children so frequently find that roaming the streets is more interesting than back yards or playgrounds? Because the sidewalks are more interesting. It is just as sensible to ask: Why do adults find lively streets more interesting than playgrounds?'* (Jacobs, 1961)

The obsessive creation of playgrounds was simply a way of segregating children (and their mothers) from the rest of society, she said. It consolidates mothers as the sole carers for their children and removes men from children's lives. It cuts them off from a source of stimulation and experimentation. It is little wonder that Jacobs didn't favour them.

Moses also built many of New York's suburbs – low-density housing accessible only by car – something Jacobs railed against and that many people consider problematic today (although many governments still build them).

Her opposition wasn't wholly based on sentiments of place, as Kanigel suggests. She believed – and this was a perspective she developed throughout her work – that segregating function and eliminating the everyday commercial possibilities of the city destroyed its economic basis and could lead to stagnation. We will return to this point in Chapter 3.

Jacobs as Influencer

Jane Jacobs was an 'outlier', a term coined by Malcolm Gladwell in his book *Outliers* (2008) to describe a person who stands against the group and forges ahead on their own, establishing new frontiers of knowledge. This was certainly true of Jacobs, so it is equally pertinent to think about the kinds of movements she influenced, as well as those who influenced her.

Jacobs had an enormous impact on the politics of cities. Toronto is probably the best example of how her ideas are manifest in a city. Not long after the Jacobs family had arrived in Canada, Bob's boss, architect Eberhard Zeidler, asked Jane for her advice on a number of his projects in Toronto. One of these was the Eaton Centre, a galleria right in the centre of downtown. Zeidler wanted to incorporate it into the surrounding city rather than it being a separate, stand-alone entity, as these shopping malls so often are.

The mayor of the city, David Crombie, was also a big fan of Jacobs (as we saw in Chapter 1). He devised a large housing

Fig. 3 St Lawrence is a development influenced by the ideas of Jane Jacobs. It has become hugely successful because of its mixed use of residential and commercial character. The buildings are dense but low-rise, the sidewalks wide and the design variable.

project on 56 acres of industrial wasteland east of downtown which would house 10,000 people. St Lawrence, as it became known, combined much of Jacobs' principles about mixing residential and commercial builds, seamlessly knitting the old neighbourhood and the new one together, creating dense, low-rise streets of flats with commercial and retail spaces below and three-story town houses. In the years since it has been a massive success, with other developments emerging along its edges and creating a thriving neighbourhood where people want to live.

In 1997, some 35 years after the housing project was realized, *The Globe and Mail* newspaper wrote an article describing St Lawrence as 'the best example of a mixed-income, mixed-use, pedestrian-friendly, sensitively-scaled, densely-populated community ever built in the province' (cited in Kanigel, 2016).

It is hard to imagine that any movement which questions big development, the building of new roads or the displacement of people has not, at some point, stumbled across Jacobs. This also goes for advocates of mixed-use street level architecture, small business and public transport. As will become evident in later chapters, when we discuss Jacobs' core concepts, groups such as these will spring up time and again, clearly indicating Jacobs' influence.

But despite working from the same principles, not everyone understands how to put them into practice. Take for example the New Urbanism movement (NU). NU is a broad-based movement that aims to promote a notion of the urban that existed before cities were shaped by the car – mixed-use neighbourhoods where homes and businesses exist together, walkable pavements and a people-centred streetscape. In fact, the sort of urban planning that Jane Jacobs might advocate.

NU emerged in the 1980s in America and was formalized in the founding of the Congress for New Urbanism (CNU) in 1993. Take a look at their founding statement overleaf.

Although this statement appears to be in line with Jacobs' philosophy, she didn't entirely agree with the New Urbanists, as is evident in an interview she gave for the magazine, *Reason*, in 2001:

> *The New Urbanists want to have lively centers in the places that they develop, where people run into each other doing errands and that sort of thing. And yet, from what I've seen of their plans and the places they have built, they don't seem to have a sense of the anatomy*

of these hearts, these centers. They've placed them as if they were shopping centers. They don't connect. In a real city or a real town, the lively heart always has two or more well-used pedestrian thoroughfares that meet. In traditional towns, often it's a triangular piece of land. Sometimes it's made into a park.' (Jacobs quoted in Steigerwald, 2001)

Other critics echoed Jacobs' criticism. DeWolf, reviewing the New Urbanism movement in 2002 for *Planetizen* – a planning-related news website owned by Urban Insight – went further. He argued that, while the aesthetics of NU was all about small-scale design, they often lapse into design nostalgia without tackling the real intent, which was to create community:

'New Urbanist towns too often commit the most heinous of urban sins: they segregate zones. Certainly, it is not uncommon to find small commercial outlets in the residential quarters of neo-traditional developments, but by and large these neighbourhoods follow the standard planning principle of the past fifty years, which is to distinctly separate zones according to use.' (DeWolf, 2002)

For Jacobs, uses should be mixed and flexible, and centres connected by well-used pedestrian routes. The NU approach, while having all good intentions, was simply overdone and over-engineered. Neighbourhoods were better when people were free to experiment according to their own needs and vision. It is this point that is absolutely crucial to understanding Jane Jacobs. Her

Founding statement of the CNU

The Congress for the New Urbanism views disinvestment in central cities, the spread of placeless sprawl, increasing separation by race and income, environmental deterioration, loss of agricultural lands and wilderness, and the erosion of society's built heritage as one interrelated community-building challenge.

- *We stand* for the restoration of existing urban centers and towns within coherent metropolitan regions, the reconfiguration of sprawling suburbs into communities of real neighborhoods and diverse districts, the conservation of natural environments, and the preservation of our built legacy.

- *We advocate* the restructuring of public policy and development practices to support the following principles: neighborhoods should be diverse in use and population; communities should be designed for the pedestrian and transit as well as the car; cities and towns should be shaped by physically defined and universally accessible public spaces and community institutions; urban places should be framed by architecture and landscape design that celebrate local history, climate, ecology, and building practice.

- *We recognize* that physical solutions by themselves will not solve social and economic problems, but neither can economic vitality, community stability, and environmental health be sustained without a coherent and supportive physical framework.

- *We represent* a broad-based citizenry, composed of public and private sector leaders, community activists, and multidisciplinary professionals. We are committed to re-establishing the relationship between the art of building and the making of community, through citizen-based participatory planning and design.

- *We dedicate* ourselves to reclaiming our homes, blocks, streets, parks, neighborhoods, districts, towns, cities, regions, and environment

work is about specificity – getting to grips with the particularity of each neighbourhood and understanding how it should work according to its own laws. There is no 'one size fits all' approach that can work, according to Jacobs. Every community is unique.

The New Urbanist dispute illustrates the difficulty of trying to neatly summarize a body of work and to a formula. Nothing of what Jacobs wrote was formulaic. It was always provisional, developing, changing and being revised. This isn't surprising as her work was based on close observation, as we have already seen. As life changes, so does insight. The challenge is in being able to confidently understand her method, apply it, and revise it for any new conditions, such as those we face today. This is what working in the spirit of Jane Jacobs really consists of.

In the next three chapters, we will look at Jacobs' work under three main concepts – diversity, density and democracy. Each of these sets out to underline how her body of work should be seen as her own individual perspective and approach that she applied to her own built environment. It is not a recipe that one can apply directly to the spaces around us, instead it is an attitude that encourages individual critical reasoning and acting upon one's own personal experience.

3. The Vital Role of Diversity

The idea of diversity has become contentious within certain sectors in the 21st century, with politicians and media from the political right railing against immigrants, multiculturalism (where people from different nationalities, cultures and faiths live side by side) and anything that causes populations to drift from what they see as the 'normal' or 'traditional' state of affairs.

However, 'diversity' has multiple meanings, as Jacobs realized. For her, diversity plays an important role in many types of things, from the nature of the built environment to a country's economy, its culture and its people. She saw diversity as a source of economic and cultural dynamism, and vital to a city's continued flourishing.

As previous chapters have illustrated, Jacobs' target of attack was the city planners who thought they could remake society through obliterating old neighbourhoods and building new ones. As she argued, 'You can't create the texture of a living city in one fell swoop that way. Things must grow' (Jacobs, 2016). This kind of organic growth implies that we celebrate diversity rather than try and remake reality through one vision of how cities should look and be.

It seems likely that Jacobs was influenced by the American philosophical tradition of pragmatism – a thread that runs through much American writing. Pragmatism simply sees thought having a strong connection to action and human reality. You can both understand reality and act upon it. Pragmatists generally argue ideas are fallible and need constant revision. The tradition also implies a liberal attachment to pluralism, whereby minority groups maintain their cultural traditions and these creative differences are valued. Engaging with reality in this way, and accepting that our understanding of it is provisional, also suggests that no one view is right. Rather, our perception of reality comes over time and in connection with different perspectives and contexts, as well as the fact that we are acting on that reality.

Jane Jacobs is often described as a person who single-mindedly believed she was right. But perhaps it would be more accurate to say that (as the previous chapter also implies) she was someone who constantly changed her ideas as new elements were brought in and as she lived through new experiences. Her approach to understanding – to read eclectically and to ethnographically engage with her environment as a researcher, writer and activist – and to somehow bring this all together, automatically lends itself to a belief in the value of diversity.

So first and foremost, her method and approach towards understanding cities and economies was about absorbing diverse life experiences and intellectual viewpoints. Nothing was denied and it was all viewed as part of a whole. This is what she said about admitting a diversity of perspectives into your worldview:

'...there are two different ways you encounter things in the world that are different. One is that everything that comes in reinforces what you already believe and what you already know. The other thing is that you stay flexible enough or curious enough and maybe unsure of yourself enough – or maybe you are more sure of yourself, I don't know which it is – that the new things that come in keep reforming your world view.' (Jacobs 2001)

The concept of diversity was a strong thread in her evolving perspectives on cities and the built environment. So what does diversity do for city economies? Let's look at the different ways she discusses diversity in turn.

The Imperfectability of the City

Jacobs did not believe that one vision of the city should hold sway. She also did not believe that the one vision should be that which tried to erase the imperfections and disorder of the city. In an interview for *Mademoiselle* magazine in 1962 titled 'Disturber of the Peace', Jacobs referred to this perspective, rife in the planners of her day, as 'grandiosity':

'The kind of planning for a city that would really work would be a sort of informed, intelligent improvisation. Which is what most of our planning in life is in any case. [...] The whole notion of simultaneous uplift for an area has nothing to do with real life or growth. And then there is this ideal involved in it: that you should make things perfect and keep them that way. Well, this is a form of death, of course.' (Jacobs, 2016)

Jacobs believed that planners thought this way because they were 'captives of their time' (Jacobs, 2001). The circles they connected with, and their training, were too narrow to allow for other possibilities. In Jacobs' time (and to some extent ours as well), the emphasis was on top-down planning – where planners, architects or government create a vision and impose it on residents without their input – and on one dominant vision. Jacobs proposed a more bottom-up approach, based on people's needs.

One of her best examples is the building model known as the Garden City. These developments were built in the UK before and after World War II (1939–45) and include Harlow, Letchworth, Welwyn Garden City and Milton Keynes. Their founder was Ebenezer Howard, author of *Tomorrow: A Peaceful*

Fig. 4 The ideal of healthy village life formed the model of the garden village common to much English housing development in the 20th century and beyond. Jane Jacobs felt they were boring and stultifying, devoid of amenities, interest and human connection. The Ebbsfleet, currently under construction in Kent, is a modern example of a garden city.

Path to Real Reform (1898), which described a utopia where people would live in harmony with nature, in contrast to the gritty urban landscapes that were forming in the UK then. Garden Cities did not grow organically; they were heavily planned, with a central retail zone surrounded by housing with generous gardens. They were inspired by the anti-alcohol Temperance Movements – you were unlikely to find a pub in one of them. These cities were heavily dependent on cars and had very little street life. In the UK, they have struggled to maintain a thriving economy (apart from Milton Keynes, which has benefitted from the employment pool created by the Open University and a thoughtful local government).

Jacobs was entirely scornful of Garden Cities, seeing them as an example of the controlling hand of planners. 'The planners of Garden Cities,' she said, 'had it all decided what [...] life should be like for people, what was and what wasn't good for them. This is true of all utopian thinking' (Jacobs, 1962).

Not only were they monocultural and just boring places to live, they were also dangerous to the future of society. Jacobs illustrated this by looking at Howard's approach to the economy. Whereas Jacobs wanted to utilize the diverse and unruly energies of the city, which she believed (and had witnessed) allowed the economy to develop, thrive and grow, Howard wanted to tame it into some kind of outdated feudalism:

> 'Howard aimed at outfoxing the bewildering new city merchants and other entrepreneurs who seemed to spring up inexhaustibly from nowhere. How to leave them no scope in which to pursue their operations, except

> *under the tight directives of a monopolistic corporate plan – this was one of Howard's chief preoccupations in devising his Garden Cities. Howard feared and rejected the energetic forces inherent in urbanization combined with industrialization. He permitted them no part in overcoming slum life.'* (Jacobs, 1961)

And what allowed cities and therefore economies, to thrive, according to Jacobs? It was their diversity and imperfectability, out of which came good ideas and innovations:

> *'I believe that lively cities where society can operate in an intense way make meetings out of which very fertile and ingenious decisions can come. But if people are isolated, fragmented, if one income class is set off from another income class, the meeting simply does not occur. If different kinds of talents don't come together, if different sorts of ideas don't rub up against one another, if the necessary money never comes into juxtaposition with the necessary vision, the meeting doesn't occur.'*
> (Jacobs, 1962)

The kind of sentiment expressed by Howard – top-down control, a paternalism which suggests he knows best – was not just to be found in the Garden Cities. In the UK, they ran across all the slum clearances and urban renewal projects of the post-World War II period (1945–79), nearly obliterating the entire Victorian housing stock and town centres in cities. Imagine what London would look like without its winding streets and alleyways, beautiful Victorian houses and commercial streets. Would those hipster businesses take off in Garden Cities such as Harlow instead?

Yet the utopian thinking that informed Howard is still around today. The UK government is currently planning a number of new towns and garden villages, where community, economy and activity is an afterthought and cars transit the central organizing concern. It is still the case that successive governments in the UK and the USA (less so elsewhere), fuelled by racism, find the diversity and disorder of the city a source of fear, no matter how much evidence there is that cities are the powerhouse of the economy and innovation.

The Meaning of Mixed Uses

We are all familiar with the struggling high street. Whether it's a deprived part of a city, which only offers betting shops and takeaways, or the financial centres of a city, which are dead outside of working hours, and where shops and restaurants can find it difficult to get enough custom to survive.

We are also all too acquainted with the blight of housing estates in the UK, and housing complexes in the USA – those warrens of concrete with no discernible relationship to their surroundings, which suffer from a lack of maintenance and community. The media often like to blame this on the inhabitants, though Jacobs would argue it's a function of how they were designed.

And lastly, there are the new-build housing developments with no shops. Even in blocks that have been built with commercial space underneath (in a nod to encouraging living/work spaces), the commercial spaces generally look empty, and therefore invite little foot-traffic (which somewhat defeats the initial idea).

The problem with all of these scenarios, according to Jane Jacobs, is that they fail to take account of how the built environment works, and how it works best. Put simply, places and commercial life work best when residents live around commercial spaces, when commercial spaces are small (so ensuring low-rent for the start-up or 'mom and pop stores' – microbusinesses run by one person or a couple lacking in up-front capital), when those commercial spaces are well-connected to paths that pedestrians use already, and where there is a good diversity of businesses to attract people for a considerable period of time.

Let's look at commercial spaces first. Jacobs argued, both in *Death and Life* and in her later works on economics, that cities were incubators for innovation. Why? Because so many people with different skills and thinking come together, sharing ideas. Small business is the engine of the city, which may evolve into larger businesses that export and extend their reach beyond the city to the regions (thus enriching the regions and rural areas too). Small business, though, lacks capital. They can't afford bespoke offices. They need old run down, low-rent places where they can establish themselves. It explains why, for example, the Elephant and Castle shopping centre in South London, which was previously run down and empty, became home to many, mostly Colombian, businesses (often places can become inhabited by one nationality or continent because those areas become sanctuaries for particular peoples). Jacobs reiterates this in *Death and Life*: 'Old ideas can sometimes use new buildings. New ideas must use old buildings'.

New buildings cost a lot to build, and when they are rented out, the landlords need to recover the costs of that build. Therefore, they will be expensive and out of the reach of small businesses. With old buildings, the capital outlay was paid off a long time ago. They are probably more dilapidated and unsuitable for shiny large businesses, hence, they rent for less. Razing old neighbourhoods to the ground and building anew escalates costs for small businesses. Jacobs describes in detail across all her work the relationship between urban renewal and the disappearance of the commercial life of a neighbourhood.

This is one meaning of the mixed-use neighbourhood – a mix of old and new buildings to encourage a diversity of commercial activity. What about others? When Jane Jacobs talks about mixed uses, she means:

> '*Flourishing city diversity, of the kind that is catalyzed by the combination of mixed primary uses, frequent streets, mixture of building ages and overheads, and dense concentration of users, does not carry with it the disadvantages of diversity conventionally assumed by planning pseudoscience.*' (Jacobs, 1961)

Planners, she argued, like a certain kind of order – they like to zone places according to use (for example, zones for commercial activity, retail, residential etc.). This is still true today, if we consider how many shopping centres and large shed-based retail outlets are still built. With residential builds, each block of houses looks much the same as the next. Local government and planners assume that streets that have a large volume of people, flats above shops, different kinds of shops and businesses (in ever-smaller microcosms of space) and a variety of building styles, are messy and 'disorderly'. Jacobs argues:

'Diversity of uses [...] while it is too often handled poorly, does offer the decent possibility of displaying genuine differences of content. Therefore these can become interesting and stimulating differences to the eye, without phoniness, exhibitionism or belaboured novelty.' (Jacobs, 1961)

Of course, city streets need to be stimulating, because this very stimulation gives people ideas, and ideas create innovation and, in turn, wealth. Mixed uses also matter because they are more likely to be neighbourhoods that don't favour the car as the primary mode of transport. Whereas monocultural uses imply that people will drive from one activity to the next. People always drive to out-of-town shopping sheds, for example. But if your grocers, your butchers, your café and pub, your art gallery and your home are more or less in the same area, aren't you more likely to walk?

A variety of buildings also matters because it can create a diversity of route. Jacobs criticized the tendency of cities to build long, monotonous blocks, because they cut off walking routes. Why does this matter? Because if people can take a variety of routes it permits chance encounters between people, which increases social complexity and the sharing of ideas, which is vital to the commercial success and social order of cities.

Lastly, Jacobs argued that commercial and retail streets need to create maximum footfall (the number of people visiting and using the services). One of the ways they can do this is by being in districts that cater for more than one social group. Take, for example, a thriving local café. They'll be providing for the morning rush hour (takeaway coffees and pastries, perhaps?), parents with young children in the late mornings and the local workforce at lunchtime. In the afternoons there may be informal café-based meetings and in the evening, the stragglers who are too tired to cook. That's a pretty busy café working to maximum capacity.

Now consider the opposite. Jacobs talks about the area around Wall Street in Manhattan, New York (the financial district), which had virtually no amenities and industry apart from the finance sector:

> '*To see what was wrong, it is only necessary to drop in at any ordinary shop and observe the mob scene at lunch and the dullness at other times [...] This degree of underuse is a miserable inefficiency for any plant.*'
> (Jacobs, 1961)

Underused businesses and retailers are unable to cover costs and so quickly go out of business or move on. As a result, areas become bleak and unused, and before long, start to feel unsafe.

The idea of successfully diverse areas raises an interesting question of how to progress an area to the point at which it stops being derelict or in decline but not to the point where it has lost its character. Can local government grants to regenerate areas help? There are many examples of good regeneration schemes or areas that have been 'gentrified'. But perhaps, Jacobs might argue, these are the ones that have been enacted by local government but without the wholesale destruction of housing, retail and other existing infrastructure.

Take, for example, Jacobs' discussion of junk yards and used-car lots, which use up large elements of land and are generally unattractive. Jacobs argued that when they spring up in abundance, it illustrates a struggling area – normally, she says, they emerge in areas where economic diversity is low. However, the solution is not to get rid of them, but to create the conditions for other businesses and uses to thrive. Her solution is to ease the controls from housing project malls so they can find their 'natural economic level', allowing for other kinds of businesses to take root and ultimately dilute unproductive uses. In other words, people will occupy spaces and create flourishing businesses as long as there are no zoning controls which prevent them from using the spaces as their needs dictate. Such activity will valorize an area and make it more economic to be rented to a range of businesses.

'Spitalfields Life' is a blog (later generating a book of the same name) that charts the historical and contemporary life of Spitalfields, London. In an interview I conducted with its author, known as The Gentle Author, we talked about the gradual erasure of small businesses from this part of the East End of London. The Gentle Author argued that eliminating small business would ultimately destroy the commercial basis of Spitalfields. Reflecting on how the situation could be saved, they argued that the solution lay in planning, to allow for genuine microbusinesses, 'because what they call small shops is not what we think of as small shops'. There also needs to be a change of thinking about the value of these long-established cultural goods:

> *'I also think there has to be some kind of protection for long-established small businesses. I think that has to*

be built into business rates and national government policy. Big companies are able to lobby and get all these concessions, but that's not happening on the other side. That's what I think would change it.'

Finally, the Gentle Author argued that business rates are not conducive to independent small business (Talbot, 2018b). Whether deliberate or not, this kind of thinking is influenced by the perspectives of Jane Jacobs and her thoughts on mixed-uses – and why they matter. Independent business and start-ups have an economic value beyond their cultural appeal. They aren't just nice things to have – without them there would be no city economy.

Social Diversity

Robert Kanigel, who wrote the first full biography of Jane Jacobs (2017), notes that six years after emigrating to Toronto, Jacobs became a Canadian citizen. During her citizenship hearing, she argued that she liked Canada's 'mosaic' idea of ethnicity. Immigrants did not need to assimilate into a 'melting pot,' as in the United States. Instead, they could hold onto their ethnic roots and their language.

Although Jacobs rarely wrote about immigration or social and ethnic diversity in great length (although she does refer to it), it seems likely that an appreciation of the benefits of immigration was intrinsic to her model of urban diversity. Cities in the United States have been made by successive waves of immigrants, each using small business as a means of self-advancement. Indeed, in many countries of the West, it is the discrimination against immigrants and minorities that has led to their setting up small businesses by way of necessity. Jacobs, for example, wrote about East Harlem in New York and the way that small businesses arose to cater for the needs of African-Americans corralled into the ghetto.

Even in the UK, which has not historically had high levels of immigration, many cities have been enlivened by the shops, cafes and restaurants set up by immigrants. Without them, it is hard to imagine what the average independent retail street would look like today.

In 2000, Jacobs directly talked about the role of immigrants in urbanism in a lecture entitled 'Time and Change as Neighborhood Allies' on the common failures of city neighbourhoods and how to change them:

> *'Right now, in locations extending from the Virginia metropolitan fringes of Washington and the Jersey metropolitan fringes of New York to the Los Angeles fringes of Los Angeles, striving immigrants from Pakistan, Bangladesh, India, China, the Philippines, Latin America, the Caribbean and Africa, are settling in woebegone city suburbs to which time has been unkind. Right now newcomers are enlivening dull and dreary shops with tiny grocery and clothing stores, second-hand shops, little importing and craft enterprises, skimpy offices and modest but exotic restaurants.'* (2000/2016)

Far from holding a moral view of immigration (though there's no doubt that she embraced a diverse and tolerant perspective intrinsic to her belief in social justice), this quote illustrates how she saw immigrants as a vital part of the economy of cities, weaving ingenuity into broken areas. She argued that the role of city governance should be to make sure those areas hold onto their diverse populations – the last thing marginal areas needed was to be seen by immigrants and residents as an area they would like to escape from as soon as they are offered the opportunity. Areas that held on to their diversity and immigrant populations over successive generations – and she cites Little Italy and Chinatown as positive examples – become 'civic assets in every respect: social, physical and economic' (2000/2016).

So what should city governments do for these areas? She said that,

> '...newly minted immigrant neighborhoods [should] receive really good municipal housekeeping, public maintenance, and community policing and justice services, along with some respectful amenities. Traffic-taming and street trees come to mind, and especially quick, hassle-free permissions for people to organize open-air markets if they ask to, or run jitney services, or make whatever other life-improving adaptations they want to provide for themselves.' (2000/2016)

Too often immigrant neighbourhoods are neglected and quickly become marginal places, no matter that they are home to the residents who live there. And, too often, authorities see immigrants as troublesome to their areas rather than an asset, and they look for a myriad of ways to move them on and close down their businesses.

For Jacobs, such actions were counter-productive and self-defeating – homogenous neighbourhoods, whether in physical or social structure, could never generate the life, amenities and economic dynamism that diversity could deliver.

Women and the City

In Chapter 1, we argue that Jacobs never directly wrote about feminism, though she undoubtedly embodied everything that the early feminists were – strong willed and with a frontier outlook. She did, however, write about women and their role in the urban and economic environment. This was, in part, because Jacobs wrote from the standpoint of 'the other'. If we consider that most planning and urbanism was (and is) written and dictated by white, middle-class men, then Jacobs offered a unique perspective as a woman with children.

In *Death and Life*, Jacobs devotes an entire chapter to looking at how children move around cities and why shunting children away from the streets and into park playgrounds may not be a good idea (because they are removed from adult oversight – the 'eyes on the street' – which we will return to in Chapter 5). Her writing on children, which we looked at in Chapter 2, is an example of both the alternative positionality she brought to urbanism and her point that we need to study the urban from the perspective of its inhabitants – how they actually use space as opposed to how planners would like them to use space.

Her writings on the economic potential of women are also remarkable and very much a forerunner of current thinking about the role of women in the developing world. In a speech for the Canadian Woman Entrepreneur of the Year Awards in 1994 entitled 'Women as Natural Entrepreneurs', Jacobs argued that one of the few ways women and immigrants have of breaking the glass ceiling is to establish their own businesses. She proposed that women were historically natural entrepreneurs, making most of the products of society, while men's work was very specialized (hunting, animal husbandry, warring, tax collecting, law, religion, for example). Most of our contemporary economy of production involves products that were traditionally women's work.

The problem arises when, once women have founded successful businesses, they are then often taken over by men – in the first instance by family members. Those businesses then very quickly become monopolized by men. Jacobs says:

> *'It isn't enough for businesswomen to establish successful companies, vital though that is. Still another step is needed. Women entrepreneurs can consciously seek, test and encourage daughters, sisters or unrelated women able to share top responsibilities with them as the enterprise develops and grows, whether the growth is modest or spectacular.'* (1994/2016)

This perspective on women in business is just another way of looking at diversity in cities. In fact, the experience of women – their advancement through entrepreneurialism – echoes that of other minorities. Diversity feeds innovation. Innovation fuels ideas. Ideas make money. All of these go into making thriving urban localities.

Is Diversity Enough?

Diversity is a core part of Jane Jacobs' perspective on cities and economy. Diversity of urban form and people were vitally important to build thriving urban areas. Ultimately, she felt that planners should develop a more humanistic and tolerant view of the city. They should not view them as chaotic and in need of more control. Rather, there was diversity in their order. As she argues in *Death and Life*:

> '*Being human is itself difficult, and therefore all kinds of settlements (except dream cities) have problems. Big cities have difficulties in abundance, because they have people in abundance. But vital cities are not helpless to combat even the most difficult of problems [...] Vital cities have marvellous innate abilities for understanding, communicating, contriving and inventing what is required to combat their difficulties [...] lively, diverse, intense cities contain the seeds of their own regeneration, with energy enough to carry over for problems and needs outside themselves.*' (Jacobs, 1961)

But diversity alone is not enough. Diversity is just one part of the reason why cities are so dynamic. Of critical importance is the second concept that we will explore in this book – density – an idea that has become more prominent over time, as the environmental pressures of a growing population has produced new innovations in living.

4. Density and Sustainable Growth

'There must be a sufficiently dense concentration of people, for whatever purposes they may be there. This includes dense concentration in the case of people who are there because of residence.' (Jacobs, 1961)

Density, for Jane Jacobs, was and is one of the four generators of diversity – the other three being a diversity of people, a diversity of buildings and short blocks with plenty of routes to ensure chance social encounters (see Chapter 3). Put simply, density means that there are a certain number of people per square kilometre (for example) – most likely as residents but also as users of a space (such as people working there). To those people who aren't actively involved in planning, architecture or urbanism, density as a concept seems very dry. Why does it matter how many people live and work within a square kilometre? Isn't the aim of humans to get away from other humans, and live in their own detached castles untroubled by the noise and behaviour of others?

Jacobs was interested in density because, for her, a concentration of people in one space meant that ideas could be exchanged and innovation generated. Further, that it would provide sufficient footfall (custom) for businesses. We will look at how Jacobs used the concept of density in more detail in the first section of this chapter, and in the second, how she, and others who have followed, linked density to economic dynamism.

In recent years, however, the concept of urban density has been growing in popularity for another reason – sustainability. Urbanization proceeded fast in the 20th and 21st centuries. As was noted in the introduction, for the first time in human history, a majority of the world's population is living in cities. By 2050, UN estimates put that figure at 66 per cent. The most urbanized continent is North America, with 82 per cent of the population residing in cities (United Nations, 2014).

These trends have raised fundamental questions about how we should be living, whether the polluting effects of car use are obliterating the social fabric and our health, and whether nations can afford to invest in proper systems of public transit. This is where density comes in, because finding sustainable ways to live is one way to tackle these problems. The second half of this chapter will look at density, sprawl, cars and the contemporary dilemmas of urbanization. We will also look at some of the contemporary debates around density and sprawl. So what is density and why does it matter?

Residential Density

We have outlined Jane Jacobs' most important use of the word density at the start of this chapter. For Jacobs, density means a concentration of people in an area. Why is this important? Primarily it is about the economy of cities. In Chapter 11 of *Death and Life*, Jacobs explores why cities have a 'need for concentration' and begins with the observation that 'probably everyone who has thought about cities at all has noticed that there seems to be some connection between the concentration of people and the specialties they can support'. In other words, residential density means a more diverse knowledge and skill set and also a greater amount of diverse businesses.

Jacobs looks at the study of John H. Denton, a professor of business at the University of Arizona in the USA, which observed that in American suburbs and British new towns it was not size of population but how they were distributed that accounted for the frequency of cultural amenities (such as shopping, art, cafes and restaurants). *The New York Times* reported of his work that the sparsely populated nature of new towns and suburbs – remember that the suburbs tend to have a wide distribution of mostly detached housing with retail concentrated in one strip mall, for example – 'produced such a thin population spread that the only effective economic demand that could exist [...] was that of the majority. The only goods and services available will be those that the majority requires' (quoted in Jacobs, 1961).

In other words, populations that are thinly distributed cannot support a diversity of businesses and culture. So in the suburbs or new towns, there may be just one theatre, one supermarket or general store and so on, because commercially that's all the population can support. Choice is limited, so business has to cater for the lowest common denominator. In cities, there tends to be a plethora of independent shops and chain stores, so people can choose whether to shop in a high-street retail chain, an independent boutique or a second-hand shop. There are enough people in a small geographical area to create the footfall to make all of these economically sustainable. In the suburbs, however, there are more likely to be only chain stores while independent businesses struggle, because there just aren't enough people to make them sustainable.

For Jacobs, this need for concentration or density also implies that buildings must be a good mix of residential and commercial, as explored in the last chapter. But no one function should take up space uselessly. Both residential and commercial buildings must be 'intensive in their use of land', she argues (Jacobs, 1961).

If high concentrations of people are the precursor to economically vibrant areas, why does it have a bad name? Jacobs argued that the various popular perspectives of planners of her day equated density with slums. Garden City enthusiasts, for example, equated high concentrations of residential dwellings with overcrowding (too many people living in one room) and designated both as problematic. For Jacobs, however, they were not the same thing. You could have high concentrations of residential dwellings (for example, low-rise flats, terraced housing or tenements) that are adequately populated but not overcrowded.

Fig. 5 Historic areas often show the dense network of shops and housing that Jacobs favoured. Neal's Yard in London, England, while it has become very tourist-orientated, is still very successful and architecturally unique.

In her chapter 'The need for concentration' in *Death and Life*, Jacobs listed areas in the United States that had high density, high diversity and vibrancy, including North Beach-Telegraph Hill in San Francisco, Rittenhouse Square in Philadelphia, Brooklyn Heights and Greenwich Village in New York. Conversely, she noted, slum areas were often associated with low densities:

> *'In Oakland, California, the worst and most extensive slum problem is an area of two hundred blocks of detached, one- and two-family houses which can hardly be called dense enough to qualify as real city densities at all.'* (Jacobs 1961)

Of course, density did not automatically produce vibrancy. In high density projects (housing estates) diversity had been 'regimented' out of the area, and density without diversity lacks the multi-generators that encourage organic growth. Similarly, she cites city neighbourhoods where the blocks were too standardized or long and there were no spaces for other uses.

Is there a formula to determine the correct density? For Jacobs there was no formula.

> *'Densities are too low, or too high, when they frustrate city diversity instead of abetting it. This flaw in performance is why they are too low or too high. We ought to look at densities in much the same way as calories and vitamins. Right amounts are the right amounts because of how they perform. And what is right differs in specific instances.'* (Jacobs, 1961)

Her approach is something of a 'suck it and see' one. For anyone who hasn't lived in a big city with lots of development, it might be difficult to understand. However, those who have will know that once an area gets popular, and more people start to move there, suddenly more shops and amenities appear. An area becomes more vibrant and richer. Then the developers move in and start building volume – lots of flats and high-rises. Is this the point at which vibrancy becomes frustrated? Jacobs argues that it is, if buildings that give an area variety get knocked down to make way for homogeneous structures so that the landscape becomes monotonous. So what works?

> *'Greenwich Village is such a place. It manages to house people at densities ranging from 125 to 200 dwelling units per acre, without standardisations of buildings. These averages are obtained from mixtures of everything from single-family houses and flats, on up to elevator apartments of many different ages and sizes.'*
> (Jacobs, 1961)

The reason it works, she argues, is that the buildings use space efficiently. Most land is used for the buildings rather than surrounding them with empty space, meaning that generosity of space and variety can be created in the buildings themselves. Successful neighbourhoods also need frequent streets rather than long blocks with no breaks, the latter creating monotony. As Jacobs explains, 'Long blocks with high ground coverage are oppressive. Frequent streets, because they are openings between buildings, compensate for high coverage of ground off the streets' (Jacobs, 1961). In total, she argues,

*'The combination of these devices – more numerous streets,
lively parks in lively places, and various non-residential
uses mingled in, together with great variations among
the dwellings themselves – creates totally different effects
from grimly unrelieved high densities with high ground
coverages.'* (Jacobs, 1961)

In other words, planners and architects can increase density while keeping variety and interest in the streets, making a dense urban life tolerable for residents.

Density has become an important issue for urbanism in recent years, as more people flock to the cities and populations grow. Unsurprisingly urbanists today have taken Jacobs' ideas and developed them. Vishaan Chakrabarti, author of *A Country of Cities: A Manifesto for an Urban America* (2013) and founder of the Practice for Architecture and Urbanism in New York, is one such thinker. He argues that residential density has got a bad name in recent years because it has become synonymous with high rises (always seen as bad). Like Jacobs, he says that some of the densest neighbourhoods consist of low-rise dwellings. He argues however that the key is to distribute density better. Cities can be devolved into smaller villages with downtown areas – places where people can live and work. This 'polycentric' (having more than one centre) model is aimed at managing density in relation to the need for human-centred living.

Density and Economic Growth

Density also matters for economic growth. Jacobs wanted to be known not just for her work on cities but also for her (arguably lengthier and more substantial) books on economics. In fact, she regarded her work on economics as perhaps more significant than her work on cities, though the two are intimately connected. As discussed in Chapter 1, she was determined to understand what the root causes of economic dynamism were – and she found her answer in cities. It was the expansion of cities that accounted for the affluence of advanced economies, she argued.

Her theory was based on the idea of 'import replacement'. In their early days, cities imported goods and services to meet the needs of the population. However, over time they began to produce these goods and services themselves. Once they had the capacity to produce, they could then begin to export to other cities. In turn, these cities would themselves learn to produce and export. According to Chakrabarti, Jacobs' theory explains what has happened in the technology industries in the States, 'in which the ability to produce goods and services that originated in Silicon Valley has regenerated worldwide, from Bangalore to Brooklyn, Houston to Haifa' (2013).

Cities are where economic dynamism happens. Let's look at the figures. In the UK, 40 per cent of total UK Gross Added Value (GAV, which is how goods and services produced by an area are measured) comes from rural areas and small towns. The other 60 per cent comes from London and other cities in the UK (Source: Centre for Cities). This shows that cities outperform more rural areas in the UK. Even so, rural areas aren't doing too badly in terms of their contribution. But is there more to it? A study commissioned by DEFRA (Department for Environment, Food and Rural Affairs) found differences between rural areas within city regions and those outside. In the former, productivity was 8 per cent higher and earnings 18 per cent higher. What this means, and this is what Jacobs also argued, is that rural areas work better when they have a relationship to a city and suffer when they are economically self-generating.

In the USA, the figures are even starker. Chakrabarti quotes data from the 2012 United States Conference of Mayors which states that 3 per cent of the US landmass (that's cities) generates 85 per cent of its Gross Domestic Product (GDP, which is the value in money of all goods and services produced in a year). Those are pretty remarkable findings, given what we know about the dominance of sprawl in the US. By building more suburbs and underfunding the cities, often for ideological reasons, the USA is literally undercutting the source of its wealth.

During the 21st century there has been an increasing amount of research on the economic power of cities, though it is noticeable that few of today's urban economists are female. As a result, it's likely that the needs of women and children (since women are still responsible for the majority of childcare in all countries), and all those who are not working in business environments may go unrepresented in city planning.

Michael E Porter, in his book *Competitive Advantage: Creating and Sustaining Superior Performance* (1998), argues that creating a dense network of talent and skills in urban locales creates greater economic growth than simply relying on individual initiative. Ryan Avent, in his book *The Gated City* (2011), proposed that when urban density doubles, productivity increases at a rate of between 6 and 28 per cent. Richard Florida studied the effects of urban density on the creative and knowledge economies in his book *The New Urban Crisis* (2017). He says that when high-skilled people and creative industries cluster (a different way of saying density) in one place, it fuels innovation and economic growth. This, in turn, creates 'superstar' cities, which outflank the rest (but which also have extremes of inequality because of escalating land and property prices). Florida has used this research to show why people in rural and suburban areas voted for Donald Trump in the 2016 US elections, and see the cities as being dominated by elites – cities are simply richer. The same dynamics could be seen in the 2016 Brexit vote in the UK.

Florida's work very much flowed from the analysis of Enrico Moretti (2013), who argued that in the context of the growth of the knowledge and innovation sectors, wages and high-skilled jobs had become geographically distributed, meaning that some areas (specifically some cities) outperformed all other areas. It all relates to the 'knowledge economy' – which includes innovation, IT, artificial intelligence, media and other intellectually based businesses. The cities that had a highly skilled population attracted these industries, which were also higher paying and which also had knock-on effects for other service jobs (if people have higher wages they tend to spend it on goods and services).

Chakrabarti summarizes the findings by saying 'when cities realize the benefits of agglomeration, heightened economic activity resulting in greater prosperity and innovation occurs again and again' (2013).

It is ironic, then, that governments tend to prioritize suburban and rural areas, which take more and produce less. Chakrabarti outlines some key figures to illustrate the detrimental consequences of governmental decisions. One of these examples is how tax revenue is distributed in the United States. He shows that 'most states with large cities give much more than they receive, while the less-urban states generally receive more than they give' (2013). He goes on to say,

> *'Imagine if this situation were simply made equitable. New York has a wish list of transportation projects that, combined, would cost about $32 billion – impossible under current conditions. At the same time, the city sends approximately $18 billion more in taxes to Albany and Washington than it receives back in federal and state spending. If there were an equal balance of payments between the city and the state and federal governments for just two years, New York could fund all of its transportation projects.'* (2013)

Many urbanists today argue that cities should be given more self-government and be permitted to set and use their own taxes. It illustrates that the nation state is no longer a functioning administrative body – city states might be the way forward.

Cars and Urban Sprawl

In Jane Jacobs' day, city planners aimed to reshape the city around the needs of the car. Much of Jacobs' activism was aimed at opposing the intrusion of expressways through city neighbourhoods. It is hard to believe from today's standpoint, where we are struggling with the damaging effects of the car in cities, that planners were so enthusiastic about embracing the car. But post-WWII, cars were an important manufacturing industry, providing highly paid jobs, high export potential, and attracting huge subsidies to build roads, especially in the USA, Japan and Europe.

As we have seen in previous chapters, for Jacobs, the problem with cars is that they destroy the fabric of the city. She explains:

> *'Traffic arteries, along with parking lots, gas stations and drive-ins, are powerful and insistent instruments of city destruction. To accommodate them, city streets are broken down into loose sprawls, incoherent and vacuous for anyone afoot. Downtown and other neighborhoods that are marvels of close-grained intricacy and compact mutual support are casually disemboweled. Landmarks are crumbled and are so sundered from their contexts in city life as to become irrelevant trivialities. City character is blurred until every place becomes more like every other place, all adding up to Noplace.'* (Jacobs, 1961)

She argues that these conditions could of course arise as a product of planning, even without the intrusion of the car. It is the car, however, and the fact that planners did not anticipate how much their over-planned cities and developments would allow the car to dominate, that was the problem she was faced with (and that we continue to be faced with today).

Giving the example of Le Corbusier's 'Radiant City', which combined skyscrapers, parks and freeways, Jacobs argued that he simply did not account for how much domestic car use would feature: 'His vision of skyscrapers in the park degenerates in real life into skyscrapers in parking lots' (1961).

But what do cars have to do with density? To understand this, it's important to understand the opposite of density – urban sprawl. Sprawl is the term used to describe a programme

Fig. 6 The above shows an expressway which runs through a city centre, intersecting it into two parts and creating a rupture for pedestrian mobility. Jacobs would have regarded this as a hideous expression of the rule of the car.

of suburban residential development, which is about creating detached housing with generous gardens. Houses are placed at some distance from each other and are often connected to retail outlets and other facilities only by road. So to get from one's house to a shopping mall, you have to drive.

A 2018 report by the Organisation for Economic Co-operation and Development (OECD) – founded in 1961 to stimulate economic progress and world trade – has suggested that low-density sprawl is the main way that cities have expanded (their analysis dates from 1990), though this tendency is uneven over the 37 OECD member countries. They understand sprawl to mean low population density, low development density or high fragmentation of cities (multiple town centres and residential housing separated from each other). The report suggests that while urban density has increased, so too has sprawl across most

OECD countries. This tendency is particularly marked in the United States, which would have come as a disappointment, if not a surprise, to Jane Jacobs.

Sprawl and density matter to transport because without a dense and concentrated population, public transport is not economically viable. Vishaan Chakrabarti (2013, 2018) proposed that 30 units per acre was sufficient density to support mass public transit systems. It seems like a lot, but he argues that 'it's not big skyscrapers, it's townhouses and brownstone buildings – the densest parts of Manhattan or Hong Kong are three, four, five times that' (Chakrabarti cited in Bull, 2018).

Sprawl encourages car use because of the distances between places and function (what places do – that is, whether they are retail or sports or residential). To show how this works, let's look at an example from North Colchester in the UK called the Northern Gateway.

Strictly speaking, the Northern Gateway is a sports project – local government is enabling the building of a large sports complex on a vacant plot – but the north of the town has been under development for some time now. The entire project features a series of estates containing three to four-bedroom homes (many detached). There are no shops or cafes on these estates. They are currently separate from each other, only joined by a large dual-lane road. The nearest supermarket is around two miles down the road, again accessible only by car (the road is possible to walk, but it is polluted and has no tree canopy to provide shade from the heat or rain). The sports facilities are at the top of the road, but they are not accessible by any attractive pedestrian route.

This development is a perfect example of sprawl. Detached homes (for the most part) are spread out over a large surface area. There aren't enough people to support a public transport system (though a bus comes occasionally) and no thought has been given to how people might get around if they don't have a car, even though there are no shops nearby. Right in the middle of it all is a huge road!

We all experience sprawl – it is right there in our towns and cities – and it is exactly what Jacobs observed when she looked at the dominance of the car. In *Death and Life*, she notes that:

> *'The interval of the automobile's development as everyday transportation has corresponded precisely with the interval during which the ideal of the suburbanized anti-city was developed architecturally, sociologically, legislatively, and financially.'* (1961)

On the destruction of Los Angeles in favour of suburbanization and sprawl, she says that:

> *'A few years ago, two parking places per apartment were considered ample for those moving back into the "city." Today the new apartment houses are providing three parking spaces per apartment, one for the husband, one for the wife, and an average of one per apartment for other household members or visitors. No fewer will do in a city where it is hard to buy a pack of cigarettes without an automobile; and when someone gives a party even an average allotment of three parking spaces per apartment becomes a squeeze.'* (1961)

Her point about how car use grows the more space you provide for them is aptly demonstrated by our society today. The more roads that are built, the more people use them, and the more congested they become. The more people use cars, the less they use public transport and so public transit is underfunded. The more people use cars, the more dangerous riding a bike becomes. So the cycle continues.

When it comes to density versus sprawl, the following statistic by Chakrabarti (2013) gives pause for thought. He has calculated that, if everyone could tolerate living in residences that had a density of 25 dwellings per acre (25 low-rise flats, for example, in an area nearly the size of a football field), the entire population of the world could fit into Texas. The rest of the world could be wilderness and farmland. That's how critical density is from the perspective of sustainability. If people value nature, it is important to not live in it.

Counteracting Sprawl in Favour of Density

Anti-city prejudice still dominates the thinking of governments and planners. The fact that governments are still contemplating building new towns in rural areas is evidence of an anti-city bias. In the UK, for instance, successive governments have refused to contemplate building into the green belt to enable London to expand (though it clearly has the capacity to do so). Some, notably in the pages of 'CityMetric', the *New Stateman*'s cities blog, have called for an end to the protected status of the greenbelt around London so that it can expand. Jane Jacobs herself noted later in her life that 'Greenbelts were mapped as barriers to city growth bursts and explosions' (Jacobs, 2004).

In other words, governments and planners would build anything – garden cities and new low-density suburbs – rather than build expanded high-density city areas.

Today, options that have been floated by campaign groups include building up density in the suburbs – more mid-rise flats, for example, and infill (filling in the gaps between housing on vacant land). Also suggested is the use of brownfield land, which is vacant land normally found in towns (but not exclusively) that may have been used for other functions, such as industrial units.

Create Streets, a lobby and campaign group in the UK, argues for the return of traditional streets of terraced housing and low-rise flats. They argue that it is both what people want and that it has been the most successful form of conurbation (meaning an extended urban area, merging towns with the suburbs of a city) in the UK so far. It is a concept they refer to as 'gentle density' (Create Streets, 2018).

Cars also take up space and add to sprawl. Chakrabarti shows that cars only appear cheaper to people because they are subsidized by government: roads and pollution management are all paid for by government, not car manufacturers. Taking into account the costs of healthcare from pollution and other pollution control measures, road spending, decreased land values (because places situated next to busy roads are less desirable], cars cost more than public transport at a ratio of 10:6.

The scale of public subsidy of roads in the USA is immense. The annual federal budget spent on the Federal Railroad Administration is $1.6 billion. $10.6 billion is spent on the Federal Transit Administration, $15.9 billion on the Federal

Aviation Administration and a whopping \$42.8 billion on the Federal Highway Administration (Chakrabarti, 2013).

Recent campaigns have focused on how cars use up space in cities. A study in Parkdale, Toronto showed that in fact only 4 per cent of people came to the shopping district by car, yet cars took up 30 per cent of road space. 52 per cent of retailers estimated that 25 per cent of their customers arrived by car, claiming that there wasn't enough car parking to accommodate this percentage. Yet as the figures above show, they have grossly overestimated (Chan et al., 2016). These figures show why retailers are often so pro-car since they (falsely) believe that many more people are reliant on the car to visit their retail outlet, getting upset with city authorities for not providing enough car parking. When in reality, the great majority of their customers arrive on public transport or on foot.

Increasingly, we are understanding that certain facts about the way we live are undeniable – the kinds of facts Jane Jacobs was arguing for 50 years ago: higher density, sociable streetscapes, priority for pedestrians and cyclists, dynamic business sectors fuelled by mixed-use living, to name a few. Yet we still fail to implement what we know.

This chapter has touched upon the degree to which governments and planners sit at odds with how people live and want to live – and how this conflict is fuelling protest from urbanists and activists. The next and final chapter will look at Jane Jacobs' support for greater democracy in planning and in how our urban environments should be shaped.

5. Democracy and Downtown

With everything that has been discussed so far, it probably seems self-evident that Jane Jacobs believed in democracy. From her activism against city planners to her belief that you need to experience places to understand them (and she urged planners to do the same), Jacobs was a vigorous supporter of democracy and freedom – particularly compared to today, where belief in, and support for, democratic ideals lies thinly on the ground.

But there is more to be said about the ideal of democracy in urbanism and its practices, and the issue is particularly relevant from today's standpoint. This chapter will look at four aspects of democratization that Jacobs talked about that matter to us in the present and in which planners and architects often fail.

The first of these is the idea that places are for people, not buildings. While this idea may seem absurd, often planners and architects behave as if people were secondary. We will look at Jane Jacobs' famous essay 'Downtown is for people' and compare it to current architectural and urbanist practice around 'smart cities'.

The second issue addresses the concept of gentrification: what Jacobs said about it in her later years, what the concept means and how it is shaping cities to the detriment of the rights (democratic and social) of its citizens.

The third looks more at ideas of bottom-up (meaning by the people) criminal justice and informal social control in Jacobs' idea of 'eyes on the street' (which in many ways is her best-known idea).

The last issue swings us firmly to the present and looks at how some urbanists and activists are urging, along with a more equitable distribution of society's resources, a democratization of planning known as 'co-creation'.

Downtown is for People

> *'Designing a dream city is easy; rebuilding a living one takes imagination.'* (Jacobs, 1958)

The essay 'Downtown is for people' is a polemic against ideology as fundamentally anti-democratic. Jacobs rails against the planners' and architects' idea of building (and, of course, urban renewal), which is to impose a 'one size fits all' and top-down vision of what they think a place should look like, as opposed to what it actually is. She argued that you can't look at models of how places should look (often derived from other national and regional contexts). You have to see what the place you are dealing with is like: 'You've got to get out and walk,' she says. 'Walk, and you will see that many of the assumptions on which the projects depend are wrong.'

People create the city and make it what it is. Jacobs explains:

> *'There is no logic that can be imposed on the city; people make it, and it is to them, not buildings, that we must fit our plans. This does not mean accepting*

*the present; downtown does need an overhaul, it is
dirty, it is congested. But there are things that are right
about it too, and by simple old-fashioned observation
we can see what they are. We can see what people like.'*
(Jacobs, 1958)

One way to think about how people make spaces is to reflect
on pathways through parks. It isn't uncommon to see a worn
grass pathway that has been made by the consistent use of people
taking that route rather than the tarmac pathway put there by the
council. If planners were sensible, they would carry out simple
research to find the public's favourite route and put a path there.

Another example is how developers of apartments often like to
put balconies on the outside of buildings. Sometimes this works
– for example, if the apartment has nice views or the balcony
is a good size. Often however, the balconies have poor views

Fig. 7 This example of a desire line shows how people create their own maps through urban
spaces. Perhaps desire lines show us that urban design should flow from people rather than being
imposed from above.

(of a bus garage or railway track), are too small for sensible use or face north, and therefore never see the sun. People then use them for storage, ruining the aesthetics of the building. A more sensible idea would be to avoid balconies altogether and instead utilize the extra space for the apartment. Decent storage could be created in the basements (along with very secure bike sheds, shared laundry facilities and other shared amenities).

There are many examples, if you look around you, of how people use spaces other than how they were intended. What they need from places becomes evident too, as it was for Jacobs.

She argues that if you look at the street from the standpoint of the pedestrian, certain factors are revealed. One such example is that the walker needs to see variety: a smattering of small alleyways, different building designs and heights, different kinds of businesses and shops, and the streets punctuated with small open spaces and visual treats. She says:

> '(T)he walkers showed a great interest in punctuations of all kinds appearing a little way ahead of them – spaces, greenery, or windows set forward, or churches, or clocks. Anything really different, whether large or a detail, interested them.' (1958)

She compares this reality of what people enjoy in streets to how the planners design buildings:

> 'They are designed as blocks: self-contained, separate elements in the city. The streets that border them are conceived of as just that – borders, and relatively unimportant in their own right. Look at the bird's-eye

views published of forthcoming projects: if they bother
to indicate the surrounding streets, all too likely an
airbrush has softened the streets into an innocuous blur.'
(1958)

But surely architects and planners don't still do this? As likely as not, today they will include people in their drawings. But they are often idealized people, not real people. Ten years ago, redevelopment plans for Kings Cross station in London showed affluent and beautiful spaces, but no sign of the large numbers of homeless people and prostitutes who gathered around Kings Cross (before they were all swept away). Most people would quite rightly argue that homelessness and prostitution are not things worth preserving. However, were those people swept up into a better life, rather than just swept on (which is what actually happened) the redevelopment of Kings Cross would have been a far more successful project, both socially and morally.

There are other ways today that architects and planners contrive to ignore people. One of these is through the concept of the smart city. According to the Royal Institution of Chartered Surveyors, a smart city 'uses digital technology to promote performance and wellbeing and to increase its ability to respond to citywide and global challenges' (RICS, 2017).

Who could be against using technology to improve urban living? Technology can be used to monitor pollution or to better allocate resources in line with shifting populations. For example, healthcare could be more efficiently distributed if local government had a faster way of finding out who and how many people in certain groups (and with likely healthcare conditions) were moving into an area. Is more pregnancy support needed? Better old age services? Technology can also help complex transport systems coordinate – something that is essential if we aspire to move more of the population out of their cars and onto public transport.

But often the concept of smart cities can have quite dystopian effects. An exhibition called Our Urban Future in 2013 by Siemens at The Crystal in the East End of London showed a simulation of what smart city living would look like. It demonstrated a person living in a high-rise apartment, ordering in services and food through an inbuilt smart communications and IT system, and even working from home. It makes you wonder if that person ever left to go for a walk!

Dae Shik Kim Hawkins, an activist from Seattle, reported in *The Atlantic* (2018), on an app designed by the city's government called 'Find it, Fix it'. The app was originally designed to make it easier for community members to report potholes and other neighbourhood problems. Instead it has become a means by which homeless encampments are reported, enabling the police and local government to quickly move them on. As Hawkins reports, homelessness has been created by the absence of affordable housing in Seattle. A high proportion of the city's homeless are black people, and nothing is being done to house them. The technology coldly and efficiently 'manages' them out of lines of sight since neither residents nor businesses are willing to have the homeless housed near them.

So although smart city technologies could be used for good, all too often they imagine a sanitized future where social problems are efficiently cleansed from the streets. The problem is made to disappear, but not solved. Jane Jacobs wanted, and imagined, a more convivial and caring future, one where the needs of everyone in the city are taken into account, opportunities are open to all, and where cities are made – organically growing – by the people themselves.

If not planned around people, cities will suffer the consequences, Jacobs said. She tied the power of community to the social and economic dynamism of the city. In *Death and Life*, she says:

> *'If self-government in the place is to work, underlying any float of population must be a continuity of people who have forged neighborhood networks. These networks are a city's irreplaceable social capital. Whenever the capital is lost, from whatever cause, the income from it disappears, never to return until and unless new capital is slowly and chancily accumulated.'* (1961)

The power of human networks discussed by Jacobs was an early forerunner of the contemporary idea of social capital, though the concept itself has a longer history and is closely tied to notions of civil society (which is how people's informal networks and groups can act as one arm of governing power). As we saw with Jacobs, the notion of people acting together was important both for her idea of government but also economy. Without people acting together, ideas and innovations would not be created. (See Chapter 4.)

Which brings us to our contemporary dilemma about how communities are being decimated and networks dispersed, often summed up in the concept of gentrification.

Gentrification: a City of Haves and Have-nots

Gentrification – which describes how areas and places are made more up-market in order to appeal to middle-class culture and tastes – was not a concept Jacobs discussed until later in her life. The reason for this absence was because when she first started writing about cities, the main issue facing her was slum clearance and urban renewal, not gentrification (which only became an issue in the 1990s).

Gentrification as a concept is absolutely central to understanding the disempowerment of citizens and the need for democratic renewal. Various writers, including Jacobs herself, have observed that growing inequality in the city and the displacement of lower income people is not helping urban culture. A diversity of people and the pluralism that represents, for Jacobs, was always central to understanding why cities are so socially, culturally and economically dynamic (see Chapter 3). Without a democratic and civic culture, which embraces differences, the city would stagnate and die.

So how did Jacobs view gentrification? She observed in *Death and Life* the tendency for areas to go through cycles of renewal and decline. Shopping streets would start off diversifying, with plenty of independent businesses, and then, as land became more valuable, blander chain stores would take over. This conversion process set the stage for their stagnation. Anyone who has lived in a fast-paced city environment will be aware of this process.

It would be another female writer, Sharon Zukin, author of *Loft Living* (1982), who would apply Jacobs' ideas to the old manufacturing spaces of New York. In the context of deindustrialization – where governments of advanced industrial economies decided to precipitate the end of old industries in favour of a service economy – empty manufacturing spaces (lofts) were taken over by artists for mixed-use studios, living and performance spaces. This culture was used by real estate to leverage an increase in the value of housing and, indeed, the lofts themselves, which were converted into high-end residential spaces. The way art and culture are used to increase the value of land has become all too familiar (which is why, unfortunately, people have come to fear alternative culture when it appears in their neighbourhood). Within the realm of urban theory, we refer to this process as the conversion of 'subcultural capital' (Talbot. 1997).

After Zukin's contribution, and numerous writing since, it has become fashionable – because of the consequences of cultural improvements in areas, such as increasing house prices and rents and driving out poorer residents – to use the term gentrification as a catch-all to describe all the ills of the contemporary city, namely the growing inequality between the rich and poor. Jacobs took a more balanced view of the process, however. She supported the idea of commercial diversity – small, independent and interesting businesses were for her how a neighbourhood recovers from decline. It was also not a bad thing, in her view, for more wealthy citizens to buy into places, because there would be more money circulating in the area. This process only went bad when it began to stamp out diversity.

Jacobs was not anti-market but nor was she for inequality. In her later writing, she wrote about the need for policies to mitigate the impact of gentrification on poorer residents (who themselves, remember, made huge contributions to the social, retail and business mix of neighbourhoods). In *Dark Age Ahead*, she noted that Manhattan in New York has been completely transformed from a poor and run-down neighbourhood to a home for the very rich. The poor have been driven out, since no one advocated on their behalf. And wherever the poorer sections of the population are driven out, and diversity becomes lessened, those neighbourhoods become less interesting to the new inhabitants:

> '*Gentrification benefited neighborhoods, but so much less than it could have if the displaced people had been recognized as community assets worth retaining. Sometimes when they were gone their loss was mourned by gentrifiers who complained that the community into which they had bought had become less lively and interesting.*' (Jacobs, 2004)

Creating affordable housing is one way that policy-makers could preserve the dynamism of neighbourhoods and mitigate inequality. Jacobs also had an interesting insight into why some housing became so hyper-inflated in price – it was because there was a shortage of the kind of housing people like. Generally, in American cities, they like Brownstone tenements and houses, and in the UK, Victorian houses and flats. In the neighbourhoods people like plenty of amenities with good transport links and good schools.

Another positive policy suggestion was to encourage people to own commercial spaces. In an interview with Roberto Chavez et al. for the World Bank, Jacobs argues that rent increases in shops force smaller retailers out in favour of big chains who can mobilize the rent. Talking about a retail street near her house in

Toronto, she said that the only independent businesses that had survived were those that owned their buildings:

> *'They were thus impervious to abruptly raised rents, but so many other convenient shops and services vanished. It made me reflect that the only security for small businesses like these is ownership of their own buildings, or else of their own space.'* (Jacobs, 2002)

The final impediment to diversity was business taxation (referred to as business rates in the UK). Jacobs wrote about the detrimental effects of business property taxation in a variety of ways, often suggesting that, for small business, there should be no tax at all. But she thought that, certainly, taxation should not be based on the value of the land or property, which actively discouraged start-ups, microbusinesses and independent retail who could not afford exorbitant rates nor could suffer the consequences of revaluations based on an increase in land values. The reason there are no independent cafes and shops in central London anymore (and it used to be full of independent businesses such as authentic Italian cafes and small fashion boutiques, for example), is because of the problem of rent and rate increases.

Areas that gentrified fast and became the preserve of a homogenous group (the rich, for example) have a tendency to become slums again, in Jacobs view. In her World Bank interview, she says that you only have to look at history and how many poor areas have what were once grand mansions and buildings. She argues that they were abandoned because they became boring:

> *'You need variety for a city neighborhood to be interesting. In cases of gentrification, after the artists come, artisans and then young professionals who also want cheap rents and whose eyes have been opened by the artists and the artisans. They wouldn't have touched it before but at this point the neighborhood is seen to be trendy and fashionable. Then comes the feeding frenzy in which people are evicted.'* (2002)

In locales such as Chelsea in London, blocks of beautiful housing remain unused because they are just investment properties or are only occupied part of the year. There is no way that such sparsely populated areas can remain economically dynamic. Should investment flee from London and properties abandoned (as happened during the two World Wars of the last century) these buildings could quite easily become slums again. As Jacobs warns us, decline is just as inevitable as renewal. Bad government can cause economic collapse. What's needed is an inclusive culture and politics, which makes room for all citizens.

Eyes on the Street

Jane Jacobs' ideas also shaped notions of criminal justice and crime prevention within urban locales. To put this into context, let's imagine that we find ourselves in the grave situation of being attacked. Would we prefer to be in a crowd of people or completely alone? Would we rather people were watching? Perhaps we might read in the newspaper a story about how someone is attacked and no one steps in. But is this just a media bias? A more common occurrence is that people will step in and step up, or will, at the very least, call the police.

The idea that being around other people is ultimately safer is central to Jacobs' idea of 'eyes on the street'. It is the democratization of criminal justice and is all about strengthening the resources of civil society to manage its own problems. So what did Jane Jacobs have to say about her concept?

The notion of safety is intertwined with her general perspective in a variety of ways. First and foremost (and the one most frequently cited) 'eyes on the street' meant the way that a busy street, with plenty of small shops with neighbourhood shopkeepers, could help police neighbourhoods. Children and other vulnerable people could always run into a friendly shop if they got into trouble. That's why busy places with mixed-use developments are always safer.

'Eyes on the street' is not only about mixed-use development, however. Also important for Jacobs is the design of blocks. Low-rise developments with windows abutting the street or road, where people mixed or children played, allowed for observation from the windows of those residences. Dwellings integrated with busy thoroughfares provided the necessary oversight to allow for safety. Segregated estates with hidden alleyways and no retail spaces did not. Estates that warehoused poorer people were not likely to be safe – mixed-income neighbourhoods were better.

As Gerda Wekerle (2000) points out, however, Jacobs lay the basis for contemporary crime-prevention thinking – which holds that you can alter the environment to make it less productive of crime, and to prevent it happening in the first place by prioritizing the more psychosocial elements of fear of crime and quality of life. In *Death and Life* Jacobs says this:

'To be sure, there are people with hobgoblins in their heads, and such people will never feel safe no matter what the objective circumstances are. But this is a different matter from the fear that bests normally prudent, tolerant and cheerful people who show nothing more than common sense in refusing to venture after dark – or, in a few places, by day – into streets where they may be assaulted, unseen or unrescued until too late.' (1961)

This statement is very typically Jacobs. Rather than dismiss concerns about crime as panic mongering, as some criminologists are wont to do, Jacobs suggests that we listen to people's fears, because they are based on real experience, and find ways to make their experience better.

If people feel unsafe in city spaces, they will use them less which, in turn, makes them less safe. Finding ways to increase safety and therefore make sure streets are populated is a priority. Jacobs argued that for a street to be well used and therefore safe, it must have three qualities.

First, there must be a clear demarcation between public space (free to use by all) and private space (owned by a private individual or company). They should not merge into one another – people like to know where they are permitted to walk and not be put off by encountering potentially private space.

Second, buildings must be orientated to the streets to increase what is called 'natural surveillance'. Third, the sidewalk (pavement) must have continuous use – if a street is lively, people living in adjacent buildings will more likely be watching.

Do suburbs fare any better? White people in North America, Australia, USA and Europe often leave cities and 'escape' to the suburbs in what is known as 'white flight'. They assume that if they live in a racially pure neighbourhood (full of white people) they will feel safer. But it is interesting to hear the voice of author Lauren Elkin, who grew up in a suburb of New York:

> '...when I go home to Long Island, I find the empty streets of my parents' neighbourhood terrifying. The very appearance of another human, walking on foot, seems out of place and menacing. I don't look out of the windows after nightfall lest I see someone lurking in the back garden, staring in at me.' (Elkin, 2016)

Compare this to her experience of the city:

> 'I felt at home in the crowds, amid the hum and the neon, with the grocery store downstairs open all night, and the Ethiopian restaurant on the corner doing great takeaway; it felt, the moment I stepped outside, like I was actually part of the world, that I could contribute to it and take from it and we were all in it together [...] psychologically, in the city, I felt I could look after myself in a way I couldn't out in the suburbs.' (Elkin, 2016)

This may seem very counterintuitive, but Elkin describes how the city gave her a feeling of freedom to walk and explore, and that freedom came from the 'eyes on the street'. In the suburbs there were no eyes on the street, and so, for a child growing up there and as an adult returning from time to time, felt unsafe and eerie.

Yet, as we all know, building a sense of community that will serve as eyes on the street is a challenge in any place, including cities. Compared to Jacobs' time, people today are cynical, overwhelmed, and too frequently used to being dismissed, as big developers and government raze their neighbourhoods and the life they have always known. As communities get decimated, so do feelings of security (the 'social capital' of these areas literally destroyed).

In the following section we will look at the issue of mobilizing communities and what democratic practitioners are trying to do to make sure communities are both involved and actively shaping their environment.

Co-creation and Resistance

Jane Jacobs' view was that people know what is best for their community. When encouraged, they know what needs to happen in that particular street or what should happen to that derelict corner. Too often in our society, people are not asked or involved in what happens to the place where they live. Or they are only asked to comment in what is a rather perfunctory consultation, designed to rubber stamp decisions already made. Jacobs experienced this kind of top-down planning and, with others, fought against it.

In recent years, however, practitioners have thought of new ways to conceptualize the importance of community involvement. Projects should not be delivered by the authorities on behalf of the community. Rather, everyone needs to work together to creatively come up with solutions to the problems facing communities. That process has been called 'co-creation'.

So what is co-creation? One project that used this method extensively was Open Works (2015) in West Norwood, London, in the UK. This was a partnership between Lambeth Council and Civic Systems Lab, a 'laboratory that designs and tests methods, strategies and systems to grow the civic economy at regional, city and local level'. Together, with 1000 residents, they co-created 20 practical projects in the area. West Norwood was traditionally a marginal and deprived area of South London more known as a bus depot than for its thriving culture. But recently, it had an influx of more affluent residents.

The project wasn't targeted toward specific groups. It was open to everyone, without qualification, and the aim was to benefit everyone in the community.

The organizers observed that some community projects achieved high levels of community participation. These tended to be activities that appealed to a broad cross-section of people, such as gardening, cooking, learning and crafts. Children's projects were also high on the list. Open Works focused on these kinds of activities. They noted that, while state support was a necessary and valuable aspect of supporting communities, top-down approaches tended to disempower people. Councils were, however, reluctant to let go of their control.

To the researchers, an entirely new way of conceiving the state's relationship to its citizens was needed. Community should be something that is created together, not imposed upon one party by another. What was needed was to create a 'dense participatory ecology' that would lead to fundamental changes in community resilience. In other words, the focus was on what it would take to rebuild civil society.

Their best-practice findings make for interesting reading. They discovered that not only did these co-creative projects build community resilience; they also evolved into the 'development of community businesses, co-operatives and hybrid ventures through platform incubation programs' (Open Works, 2015). Rebuilding the basis for civil society also revitalized the local economy. It is almost as if Jane Jacobs found her way to West Norwood, so embedded in her ideas was the project.

Another way of thinking about community collaboration is through the use of charrettes. Charles Campion, partner at JTP Architects in the UK, and author of *20/20 Visions: Collaborative Planning and Placemaking* (2018), describes charrettes as:

> '…*an intensive, collaborative planning process in which designers, the community and others work together to create a vision for a place or development. The concept of placemaking is used as a lens through which to assess issues and propose actions – not just for physical plans, but for social and economic solutions too.*' (Campion, 2018)

One example of a successful charrette in action was the building of a new community on the site of a former wood mill in East Fraser, Vancouver, Canada. The proposals – for 7,000 new homes on 53 hectares of land – had been very controversial and residents were concerned about traffic and infrastructure needs such as schools and parks. A week-long charrette was organized with DPZ, a Florida-based New Urbanist practice, and a large group of residents in order to discuss various issues from transport to design. Together they came up with five designs, and from this a local architecture firm chose and worked up one of the designs, and then took it through planning. Today the community is successful, vibrant and popular.

These examples show the power and possibilities of working with communities. Jane Jacobs had to fight to be heard. Some 50 years later, we can surely do better.

The idea of democracy permeates everything Jane Jacobs wrote about. It should be obvious that it is people who make society, politics and economy, but our leaders sometimes act as though guided by a higher hand (the 'invisible hand' of the market, for example, and other forces outside of their control). Jacobs demonstrated how human society is made by people and that we, the people, have the power to make our societies better.

Conclusion

We live in a world of considerable disarray and confusion, not least in how we should organize our cities. People scramble around for a renewed idealism. On one side of the fence, architects build glittering glass skyscrapers as temples to global finance or burrow under multi-million-pound houses to add another layer of luxury to their already well-furnished homes. In this agenda, urban design seems ever more divorced from the practical reality of people's lives or from the social objectives of equality and fairness. On the other side, opponents of gentrification put their faith in social housing as a means to alleviate poverty and dislocation (which is only half of the issue – housing won't tackle poverty unless there are jobs). We do not seem to be able to settle on a sustainable plan.

Thomas Campanella, writing in *Places Journal* in 2011, lamented the loss of belief in the efficacy of urban planning even as he acknowledged its failures:

> *'Like a well-meaning surgeon who botches an operation, planners were (correctly) blamed for the excesses of urban renewal and many other problems then facing American*

cities. But the planning baby was thrown out with the urban-renewal bathwater. And once the traditional focus of physical planning was lost, the profession was effectively without a keep. It became fragmented and balkanized, which has since created a kind of chronic identity crisis – a nagging uncertainty about purpose and relevance.' (Campanella, 2011)

He noted than even Jacobs herself who, he argued, did more than anyone to throw the planning profession into doubt, grew frustrated with the timidity and lack of intellectual leadership among planners. Campanella argues that planners these days need to be better educated. They need to be able to understand the urban environment better – its physical forms, its ecology and how the 'social' (our society) works. They need to better grasp the fundamentals of architecture and engineering.

But it is more than simply providing leadership. Planning and urbanism reflects the crisis we are currently experiencing in advanced democracies around the world. The loss of purpose and idealism has translated into a cynical assault on democracy and a celebration of autocracy. Within urbanism, this is a culture war on the cities themselves, which is entirely self-defeating, since it is the cities that effectively power our economic growth. Cities face the harshest public spending cuts and the most punitive rhetoric against diversity and the freedoms of the urban environment, while resources are funnelled out of cities to maintain less well-functioning areas.

In the UK, while London's City Hall powers ahead with experiments in urban living, culture and building, borough councils – from Southwark to Waltham Forest – engage in over-development and social displacement in their own areas. Elsewhere land is concreted over and buildings entirely devoid of imagination are imposed upon the landscape, then given the name of 'new towns' and 'garden settlements'. In Sheffield, UK, against widespread local resistance, the city council has destroyed swathes of mature trees that made the city green and pleasant.

America has often led the way in urbanism, having thriving popular news outlets about cities and towns. Two worth mentioning are CityLab and Strong Towns. New Zealand is leading the way in attempting to understand the role that diversity is – and should – play in planning, through organizations such as Women in Urbanism Aotearoa and Indigenous Urbanism. China, with its rapid urbanization programme, has been forced to confront the need for advanced ecology in city planning. Globally, we have a festival of diverse viewpoints and more knowledge about how to organize our urban (and rural) societies than ever before.

In the UK, the language around planning cities, towns and rural areas is mired in ideology. Evidence and expertise are cast aside in favour of visions that either refuse to believe the state could play a positive role in building, or that the private sector has anything to offer. Jane Jacobs, of course, always argued that both had a role to play – it was a question of how they worked together and whether the people have true oversight. But city governments and planners are still reluctant to engage with the people or small-scale practitioners, preferring to deal with the few but large housebuilding firms (of which there are only five in the UK) and consultants.

Unsurprisingly, citizens respond in kind, embracing a 'not in my backyard' (NIMBY) mentality wherever new housing is proposed. But often this opposition is also promoted by the poor quality of new development. Why are they so poor? It's because there is so little competition between the limited number of developers, because housing is built for profit alone and because local authorities are underfunded and have limited oversight. Many towns in Europe, North America and Australasia are littered with faulty housing and ugly out-of-town shopping developments, and people are still wedded to their cars as we respond by building even more roads.

In many countries and cities today there is a trust deficit – in politics and in more specific areas like urban planning. Citizens of every level of wealth and expertise, and from all the many different cultures and backgrounds that make up a city's population need a greater role and input into how their neighbourhoods are planned. Citizenry needs to be considered in the round. Only recently have we understood, as noted in Chapter 1, that women's experience in urban contexts is different from men's, that the experience of immigrants is different from natives, and so on. Suffice to say that we need to understand and accept pluralism (where diverse views and perspectives can coexist) and how difference can be creative. Planners need to trust that, given appropriate powers, the voice of the people will be constructive rather than rejecting.

Importantly, one could argue that we need to focus more on evidence than ideology. Even with a pragmatic and intellectual magpie like Jane Jacobs, some people are apt to turn her writings into a set programme, appropriate for all times and contexts. It is important to keep an open mind and be led by competing evidence in deciding how a particular project should work. As Vishaan Chakrabarti argues, sometimes tower blocks might be the most appropriate way of building – whether they work depends on the context they are in and how they are built.

Hopefully, *Who the Hell is Jane Jacobs?* has given you, our reader, an insight into who Jacobs really was and how her ideas developed over the course of her life. What she has given us is, not a toolkit, but an introduction to a way of thinking and a way to approach the fundamental problems of the city. Like Jacobs herself, we should question her ideas – we can take some of what she argued, but also be free to reject others as inappropriate for our times.

Importantly, though, the task of interpreting them and how they might work in the places you live is up to you. Jane Jacobs would have argued that you should take a walk around your neighbourhood and see how it feels. Read up on economic statistics and local stories. Think about what you might do in that neglected bit of space. Above all, know that you should have an opinion about where you live. Urbanism shouldn't be an elitist and remote profession. Urbanism is about life, politics and citizenship and it affects us all.

Bibliography

Works by Jacobs

Jacobs, J. (1940) *Constitutional Chaff*. New York: Columbia University Press.

Jacobs, J. (1958) 'Downtown is for people', Fortune, April 1958, in Zipp, S. and Storring, N. (eds). *Vital Little Plans: the short works of Jane Jacobs*, New York: Penguin Random House.

Jacobs, J. (1961) *The Death and Life of Great American Cities*, New York: Vintage Books (this edition 1992).

Jacobs, J. (1962) 'Disturber of the Peace: Jane Jacobs', Interview with Eve Auchincloss, *Mademoiselle*, in *Jane Jacobs and Other Conversations* (2016), Brooklyn, New York: Melville House Publishing.

Jacobs, J. (1969) *The Economy of Cities*, New York: Vintage Books.

Jacobs, J. (1984) *Cities and the Wealth of Nations*, New York: Vintage Books.

Jacobs, J. (1992) *Systems of Survival: A Dialogue on the Moral Foundations of Commerce and Politics*, New York: Vintage Books.

Jacobs, J. (1994) 'Women as Natural Entrepreneurs' in Zipp, S. and Storring, N. (eds). *Vital Little Plans: the short works of Jane Jacobs*, New York: Penguin Random House.

Jacobs, J. (2000) *The Nature of Economies*, New York: Vintage Books.

Jacobs, J. (2000/2016) 'Time and Change as Neighborhood Allies', Vincent Memorial Prize Lecture, National Building Museum, Washington D.C., in Zipp, S. and Storring, N. (eds). *Vital Little Plans: the short works of Jane Jacobs*, New York: Penguin Random House.

Jacobs, J. (2001) 'Godmother of the American City', Interview with James H. Kunstler, in *Jane Jacobs and Other Conversations*, Brooklyn, New York: Melville House Publishing.

Jacobs, J. (2004) *Dark Age Ahead*, New York: Vintage Books.

Jacobs, J. (2016) *Vital Little Plans: The Short Works of Jane Jacobs*, New York: Random House.

Jacobs, J. (2016) *Jane Jacobs: The Last Interview*, New York: Melville House Publishing.

Other works cited

Alexiou, A.S. (2006) *Jane Jacobs: Urban Visionary*, New Brunswick: Rutgers University Press.

Avent, R. (2011) *The Gated City* (e-book) Available at: https://www.amazon.com/gp/product/B005KGATLO/ref=as_li_qf_sp_asin_il_tl?ie=UTF8&camp=1789&creative=9325&creativeASIN=B005KGATLO&linkCode=as2&tag=theurban-20&linkId=HVTX7VZ5NIDQSTOT. [Accessed 26 June 2018].

Bull, G. (2018) 'The Dense City Question' *RICS: World Built Environment Forum* Available at: https://ww2.rics.org/uk/wbef/markets-geopolitics/the-dense-city-question/?utm_source=twitter&utm_medium=social&utm_campaign=wbef. [Accessed 19 July 2018].

Campion, C. (2018) *20/20 Visions: Collaborative Planning and Placemaking,*. London: RIBA Publishing.

Campanella, T. (2001) 'Jane Jacobs and the Death and Life of American Planning'. *Places Journal,* Available at: https://placesjournal.org/article/jane-jacobs-and-the-death-and-life-of-american-planning/. [Accessed 27 July 2018].

Chakrabarti, V. (2013) *A Country of Cities: A Manifesto for an Urban America*, New York: Metropolis Books. Chan, M., Gapski, G., Hurley, K., Ibarra, E., Pin, L., Shupac, A. & Szabo, E. (2016) 'Bike Lanes, On-Street Parking and Business in Parkdale: A study of Queen Street West in Toronto's Parkdale Neighbourhood', Toronto, Ontario.

Chavez, Roberto, Tia Duer, and Ke Fang (2002) 'Urban Economy and Development: Interview of Jane Jacobs', Transcript, World Bank, 4 February 2002.

Citizen Jane (2016) *Citizen Jane: Battle for the City*, Altimeter Films.

Create Streets (2018) 'Does London benefit from over 500 tall buildings 'in the pipeline'? Is this the best way to deliver new homes?' Available at: http://www.newlondonarchitecture.org/docs/nicholas_boys_smith_createstreets.pdf. [Accessed 19 July 2018].

DeWolf, C. (2002) 'Why New Urbanism fails', *Planetizen*. Available at: https://www.planetizen.com/node/42. [Accessed 8 June 2018].

Elkin, L. (2016) *Flâneuse: Women walk the city in Paris, New York, Tokyo, Venice and London*, London: Chatto & Windus.

Florida, R. (2017) *The New Urban Crisis*, New York: Basic Books.

Gladwell, M. (2008) *Outliers: the story of success*, New York: Penguin Books.

Gratz, R.B. (2011) 'Jane Jacobs and the Power of Women Planners', *CityLab* Available at: https://www.citylab.com/equity/2011/11/jane-jacobs-and-power-women-planners/502/. [Accessed 16 July 2018].

Hawkins, D.S.K (2018) 'An app for ejecting the homeless', *The Atlantic*, Available at: https://www.theatlantic.com/amp/article/563849/?__twitter_impression=true. [Accessed 30 June 2018].

Howard, E. (1898) *Tomorrow: A Peaceful Path to Real Reform*, London: Swan Sonnenschein & Co.

Johnston-Zimmerman, K. (2018) 'Ted X – What does a female future look like in our cities?' Available at: https://www.youtube.com/watch?v=EuCTQ1PcnZ8, [Accessed 16 July 2018].

Kanigel, R. (2017) *Eyes on the Street: The Life of Jane Jacobs*, New York: Vintage Books.

Martin, D. (2006) 'Jane Jacobs, Urban Activist, is Dead at 89', *The New York Times*   https://www.nytimes.com/2006/04/25/books/jane-jacobs-urban-activist-is-dead-at-89.html. [Accessed 18 August 2018].

Miranda, P. and Powell, M. (2013) *Our Urban Future*, London: Booklink.

Moretti, E. (2013) *The New Geography of Jobs*, New York: Mariner Books.

Open works (2015) 'Designed to scale: mass participation to build resilient neighbourhoods', Available at: https://issuu.com/participatorycity/docs/designed_to_scale_v.1. [Accessed 27 July 2018].

OECD Available at: https://read.oecd-ilibrary.org/environment/rethinking-urban-sprawl_9789264189881-en#page13. [Accessed 25 July 2018].

Porter, M.E. (1995) 'The competitive advantage of the inner city', *Harvard Business review*. May–June, Available at: https://hbr.org/1995/05/the-competitive-advantage-of-the-inner-city. [Accessed 26 June 2018].

Porter, M.E. (1998) *Competitive Advantage: Creating and Sustaining Superior Performance*, New York: Free Press.

Royal Institution of Chartered Surveyors (2017) 'Smart Cities', Available at: http://www.rics.org/uk/knowledge/glossary/smart-cities/. [Accessed 30 June 2018].

Statista (2018) 'Automotive Industry', Available at: https://www.statista.com/statistics/200002/international-car-sales-since-1990/. [Accessed 16 July 2018].

Steigerwald, B. (2001) 'City Views: Urban studies legend Jane Jacobs on gentrification, the New Urbanism, and her legacy', *Reason*, Available at: https://reason.com/archives/2001/06/01/city-views/1. [Accessed 8 June 2018].

Talbot, D. (2007) *Regulating the Night: Race, Culture and Exclusion in the Making of the Night-time Economy*, Aldershot: Ashgate Publishing Ltd.

Talbot, D. (2018a) 'Small business is the engine of the city', *Forbes*, 5 June 2018 Available at: https://www.forbes.com/sites/deborahtalbot/2018/06/05/small-business-is-the-engine-of-the-city/#39694ada1eda. [Accessed 18 July 2018].

Talbot, D. (2018b) 'When small business and the financial sector collide', *Forbes*, 14 June 2018, Available at: https://www.forbes.com/sites/ deborahtalbot/2018/06/14/when-small-business-and-the-financial-sector- collide/7/#6a0415bd60d2. [Accessed 17 June 2018].

The Gentle Author (2013) *Spitalfields Life: In the midst of life I woke to find myself living in an old house beside Brick Lane in the East End of London*, London: Saltyard Books.

Ulrich, L.T. (1976) 'Vertuous Women Found: New England Ministerial Literature, 1668-1735', *American Quarterly*, Vol 28, pp. 20–40.

United Nations (2014) 'World urbanization prospects. United Nations Department of Economic and Social Affairs', Available at: https://esa.un.org/ unpd/wup/publications/files/wup2014-highlights.pdf. [Accessed 20 June 2018].

United Nations (2017) 'World Population Prospects: Key Findings and Advance Tables', United Nations: UN Department of Economic and Social Affairs.

Wekerle, G. (2000) 'From eyes on the street to safe cities', *Places*, Vol 13(1). Available at: https://placesjournal.org/assets/legacy/pdfs/from-eyes-on-the- street-to-safe-cities.pdf. [Accessed 10 July 2018].

White, R. (2012) 'New RIBA stats show large drop in women architects', *Architects Journal*, Available at: https://www.architectsjournal.co.uk/home/ new-riba-stats-show-large-drop-in-women-architects/8625001.article. [Accessed 16 July 2018].

Whyte, W. H. (1956) *The Organization Man*, Philadelphia: University of Pennsylvania Press.

Whyte, W.H. (1980) *The Social Life of Small Urban Spaces*, New York: Project for Urban Spaces Inc.

Zukin, S (1982/9) *Loft Living: Culture and Capital in Urban Change*, California: University of California Press.

Biography

Deborah Talbot is a journalist and writer specializing in urban and rural economies, development and culture. As a journalist she has published articles on transport, housing, urban economies, the rural creative and artisanal economy, sustainability and urban diversity in the following publications: Forbes CityMetric, InMotion Magazine, Reclaim Magazine, Dilettante Army and Inside Housing. She is the author of Regulating the Night: Race, Culture and Exclusion in the Making of the Night-time Economy (2007) and has co-authored and co-edited two other books. In her spare time, she enjoys urban and rural psychogeography, posting on Instagram @creativejournal_ne and Twitter @DeborahHTalbot.

Acknowledgements

Thank you to Alice Bowden and Sarah Tomley for their brilliant advice, editing and patience

Picture Credits:

Fig. 1 'Jane Jacobs in New York in 1961', available in the public domain via WikiCommons. **Fig. 2** 'Manhattan', courtesy of Pixabay: Wiggijo. **Fig. 3** 'St Lawrence', courtesy of Christopher Kowal. **Fig. 4** 'The Ebbsfleet, Kent', courtesy of Ebbsfleet Development Corporation. **Fig. 5** 'Neal's Yard in London, England', courtesy of Pixabay: Natassssa. **Fig. 6** 'Expressway which runs through a city centre', courtesy of Pixabay: Pexels. **Fig. 7** 'Example of a desire line', courtesy of Gareth M. Jones.

Who the hell is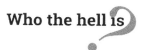

This exciting new series of books sets out to explore the life and theories of the world's leading intellectuals in a clear and understandable way. The series currently includes the following subject areas:

Art History | Psychology | Philosophy | Sociology | Politics

For more information about forthcoming titles in the Who the hell is...? series, go to: **www.whothehellis.co.uk**.

If any of our readers would like to put in a request for a particular intellectual to be included in our series, then please contact us at **info@whothehellis.co.uk**.

Printed in Great Britain
by Amazon

48061826R00067